Some of the delights of Napa Valley

1 Chateau Montelena
The iconic winery founded in 1882 (see page 97)

2 Diamond Creek
The jewel of Diamond Mountain (see page 92)

3 The Culinary Institute of America at Greystone
A centre of culinary excellence in the spectacular former Christian Brothers winery (see page 107)

4 Charlie's
High-energy restaurant from Elliot Bell, formerly of The French Laundry. A winemakers' hangout (see page 194)

5 Inglenook
Francis Ford Coppola's historic winery (see page 130)

6 Opus One
'A citadel on a hill' celebrating the Mondavi-Rothschild alliance (see page 116)

7 Oakville Grocery
A Napa Valley landmark since 1881 (see page 161)

8 Downtown Napa tasting rooms
Explore a dozen wineries within a few blocks of buzzing Napa City (see page 98)

All prices are correct at time of going to
press, but are subject to change.

Published 2025 by Académie du Vin Library Ltd
academieduvinlibrary.com
Founders: Steven Spurrier and Simon McMurtrie

Publisher: Hermione Ireland
Series editor: Adam Lechmere
Copy editor: Margaret Watmough
Design: Martin Preston
Maps supplied by Cosmographics
Index: Helen Peters
Proofreader: Jenny Sykes
ISBN: 978-1-9170-8460-4
Printed and bound in the EU
© 2025 Académie du Vin Library Ltd

All rights reserved. No part of this publication may be
reproduced, stored in a retrieval system, distributed
or transmitted in any form or by any means, including
photocopying, recording or other electronic or
mechanical methods, and including training for
generative artificial intelligence (AI), without the
prior written permission of the publisher. Translation
into any other language, and subsequent distribution
as above, is also expressly forbidden, without prior
written permission of the author and publisher.

Napa Valley
Maria C Hunt

THE SMART TRAVELLER'S WINE GUIDE

Contents

Foreword   8

● Map of Napa Valley   10
Introduction   12

● History   14
Geography   30

● Napa Valley AVAs and their wines   36

● The grapes   54
10 historic Napa wines   62

● Towns of Napa Valley   68
Visiting Napa Valley   78
Wine routes   90
How to visit an elite winery   112

see p85   see p111

The Guide 122
   Napa Valley winery tours and tastings 124
   Napa Valley hotels for wine lovers 136
   Fine dining in Napa Valley 148
   Napa Valley wine shops 158
   Napa Valley wineries with great food 170
   Napa Valley wine bars 182
   Downtown Napa tasting rooms 192

Glossary 200
Further reading 202
Index 204
Acknowledgements 208

see p136 see p182

Friedensreich Hundertwasser's brilliantly eccentric design for Quixote Winery in Stags Leap District (p132)

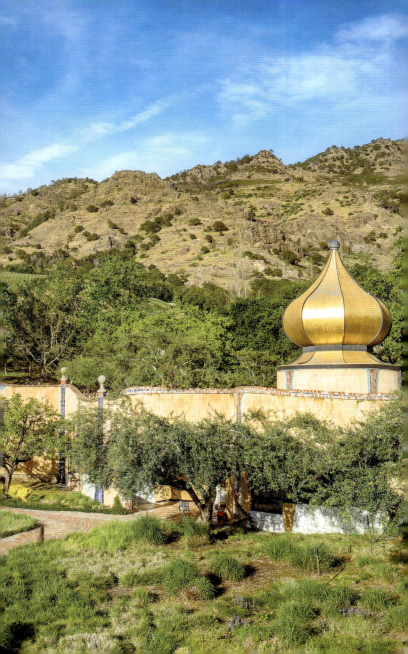

The Grape Crusher – bronze sculpture by Gino Miles, Highway 29 south of Napa

Foreword

The Napa Valley, for all its fame, is a very young region. The first wine grapes were planted here in the 1830s, and over the next five decades more than 150 wineries opened.

This rapid growth was cut short by the scourge of phylloxera, and Prohibition, but the rebirth of Napa Valley in the second half of the 20th century represented development unparalleled in any other wine region. During this era, ambitious vignerons focused on making nuanced and elegant wines that consistently rivalled the great wines of Europe.

The valley took centre stage after the 1976 Judgement of Paris; the implementation of the AVA system in the 1980s meant further recognition. From volcanic mountain soils to alluvial benchland, the world was now able to taste singular expressions of Napa Valley terroir. Our unique climate, with its extreme shift of day and night temperatures, gives us sun-kissed wines with acidity, balance and freshness.

Then came the birth of the so-called 'cult wineries': Harlan, Dalla Valle and Screaming Eagle among many others. This was in many ways due to Robert Parker's accolades. It placed us on the same level as the great châteaux of Bordeaux, but it also ushered in an era of monotony in style and structure.

But we are quick learners. The current generation takes inspiration from the past as it charts the course for the future. Young winemakers explore the history of the region through the discovery of unsung heroes like Lee Stewart of Souverain and Fred McCrea of Stony Hill; they eschew an overly opulent style and focus on more linear, balanced terroir expressions. There's a renewed interest in making wines that resemble those that built Napa Valley's reputation in the 1970s. This exciting new movement has cemented the conviction that our future must be rooted in what has gone before.

Napa Valley today is a region of spectacular beauty, its winemakers supremely confident in their craft, its wines as delicious as they have ever been. And with that confidence comes an old-fashioned open-armed American welcome, whether you're visiting a mom-and-pop farm or a winery famed around the world. There's never been a better time to discover the delights of Napa Valley.

Carlton McCoy Jr, MS
CEO, Lawrence Wine Estates

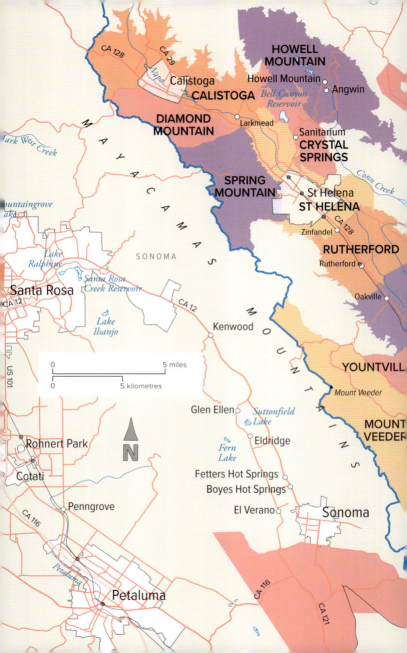

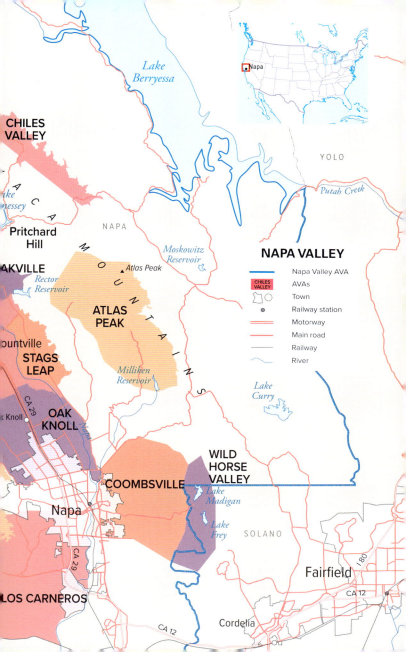

Mist over Rutherford AVA, Napa Valley

Introduction

To those who don't know much about it, the Napa Valley is a playground for the well-heeled: show-off wines, five-star hotels and exclusive restaurants. All that is easy to find (as it is in many of the world's renowned wine regions) but there's so much more to this slice of California than razzmatazz and riches.

The valley is famous for a reason. Apart from its spectacular beauty, every aspect of terroir – that magical combination of soil, elevation, climate and human intervention – is aligned here. Napa Valley has complex soils; it has rain in winter and long, dry summer days with that crucial temperature drop at night (you'll need a sweater even in August), which means deliciously ripe wines with brisk, refreshing acidity.

Sure, there's no shortage of expensive wines – this is some of the costliest vineland in the world, after all. But get off the main routes, head to the foothills of the Mayacamas in Rutherford where you'll find woman-owned Tres Sabores (p129), or out to Coombsville to taste at Favia (p121) where Annie Favia Erickson will send you home with organic tea after you've tasted her husband Andy Erickson's elegant, modern wines.

In this book we'll tell you how to visit elite wineries like Opus One (p116) and Promontory (p117) and see the Persian columns of Darioush (p135); we'll point you towards the best burgers, where to get a game of pool in St Helena, and where to find a hotel that won't break the bank. Then there are the tasting rooms in buzzy downtown Napa, and contemporary art at Copia or the di Rosa Center (p108-109), and a host of other attractions beyond wine.

The Smart Traveller's Wine Guide is for those who already love the Napa Valley and want to find out more, and for those who have that treat in store. As Carlton McCoy says in his foreword, there's never been a better time to visit.

History

Napa Valley became synonymous with fine wine thanks in large to enterprising European immigrants. But for thousands of years, the valley that stretches from the foggy hills of Carneros to the soaring forests of Calistoga was a paradise for indigenous peoples.

Downtown Napa c. 1910

Pre-historic Napa Valley: 'beautiful land'

For more than 10,000 years the valley's earliest inhabitants were a people called the Onasatis. Their beloved Napa Valley was called Talahalusi, which means 'beautiful land.' The Onasatis farmed and enjoyed plentiful seasonal foods, including acorns, wild grapes and berries, salmon, abalone and clams, and game from the forest. They crafted black obsidian glass from ancient volcanic eruptions into arrowheads and knives.

It was an idyllic life that changed dramatically in the 1820s when Jesuit priests and missionaries arrived, followed by explorers and soldiers from Spain and Mexico. These Spanish-speaking invaders called the Onasatis 'Guapo' (handsome), which became Wappo in English. Along with religion and gifts, these newcomers brought smallpox and violence to Napa Valley's native peoples. Mexican General Mariano Guadalupe Vallejo waged war on the Wappo and Pomo for a year before signing a peace pact in 1836. The very next year, smallpox wiped out more indigenous people. In the 1850s, the military organized focused attacks on the Wappo to forcibly remove them from their lands.

The 1800s: The wine pioneers

Most of the names of towns, wine regions and streets in Napa Valley are rooted in local history. The first wave of settlers to lay the foundation for the wine industry arrived in the mid-1800s.

One of the most important was George Calvert Yount. After a business setback in Missouri, Yount, a farmer, left his wife and three children to seek his fortune, arriving in California in the early 1830s. Largely due to his friendship with General Vallejo, for whom he had worked as a carpenter, Yount became the first US citizen to obtain a California land grant from Mexico. He named his 4,856 hectare estate Rancho Caymus, and in 1839 was the first to plant Mission grapes: the first *vitis vinifera* in the region. The town of Yountville, where he is buried, is named after him.

Nathan Coombs   George Calvert Yount

Nathan Coombs, another important figure, was about 20 when he arrived from Massachusetts by way of the Russian River Valley. He planned the city of Napa in 1847, and is remembered in the name of the Coombsville wine region.

Gold Rush: The Boom years

California in the first half of the 19th century was very much the wild – and unpopulated – west, but all this was to change with the Gold Rush of 1848. In the space of about two years, the population of San Francisco increased from 1,000 to 25,000. Napa Valley's wine industry boomed, driven by a new wave of entrepreneurs: men like the Prussian immigrant Charles Krug, who wed Carolina Bale, the daughter of a prominent Napa Valley family, and was given just over 200 ha of land as her dowry. The enterprising Krug planted a vineyard and founded Napa Valley's first commercial winery in 1861. He made history again in 1882, when he opened California's first tasting room. For the first time, visitors could come and sample the wine in Napa Valley.

Krug's success inspired many others. Jacob Schram, a German immigrant from Rheinhessen, bought 81 hectares on Diamond Mountain, planted a vineyard and later built a stately Victorian home. Another adventurer, the Finnish sea captain and fur trader Gustave Niebaum, founded Inglenook in 1879 and built the splendid winery that remains a Napa Valley landmark (now owned by Francis Ford Coppola, who is much admired for reviving one of the valley's great wines).

But the most important early figure was Henry Walker Crabb. The Ohio native was a natural marketing genius who cemented the Napa Valley's early status as a cradle for some of the finest wines in the world. In the late 1860s, Crabb bought 97 hectares of Yount's Rancho Caymus in Oakville. He initially planted sweet table grapes and nut trees, but in 1872 he pivoted. He renamed his vineyard Hermosa, which means 'beautiful' in Spanish, and planted vines for wine. He acquired another 145 hectares and planted more grapes. By the 1880s Crabb was growing hundreds of grape varieties including Zinfandel, Riesling, Mondeuse (which he dubbed Crabb's Black Burgundy) and Cabernet Sauvignon. The *Chicago Tribune* called him 'The Wine King of the Pacific Slope.'

Crabb's most brilliant marketing move came in 1886, when he rebranded his vineyard To Kalon. As he explained to a journalist: 'The name To Kalon is Greek and means the highest beauty, or the highest good, but I try to make it the

To Kalon Winery Depot c. 1891

boss vineyard.' And he did, winning awards and bottling more than 200,000 gallons of wine a year by 1878, putting him on an equal footing with Krug and Schram.

By this stage Napa Valley's wines were gaining international recognition. Crabb's To Kalon wines won national and international awards; Inglenook was decorated at the 1889 Paris Exposition. By the end of the decade, historian Charles Heintz notes that there were 165 wineries in Napa Valley and more than 8,000 hectares under vine. The future seemed bright, but unimagined challenges were in store.

1900s–1940: Devastation

As the wine industry boomed, more and more people came to Napa Valley and planted vineyards. As recession hit, the new plantings caused a glut of grapes and prices fell.

Phylloxera, which had first appeared in the Valley in the 1860s, began to cause serious problems. Most scientists agree that this microscopic root louse first appeared on the east coast and made its way to California on plants and farming equipment carried by settlers. While native American grapevines were immune, phylloxera attacked European *vitis vinifera*, boring into the roots of the popular Mission variety and eventually killing the vine.

About 80% of Napa Valley's vineyards died and had to be replanted. Growers who stayed afloat followed Bordeaux's example, planting disease-resistant American rootstock and grafting on European *vitis vinifera* vines to bear the fruit needed to make wine. Georges de Latour, owner of Beaulieu Vineyard, was a pioneer of this method.

Other setbacks dealt blows to Napa Valley's burgeoning wine industry. The great San Francisco Earthquake of 1906 was felt as far away as Napa Valley; the devastating fire that followed destroyed 80,000 barrels of Californian wine stored at a central warehouse in the city.

However, the biggest blow to Napa Valley was Prohibition. The Volstead Act, which came into force on 17 January 1920, banned the manufacture, sale, and transportation of

By the end of Prohibition, only a handful of Napa Valley wineries were still operating

alcoholic drinks nationwide. Vineyards across the region were abandoned and most wineries closed down.

But there were a few exemptions to the Act, and some winemakers found creative ways to survive. Beaulieu Vineyard already had a contract to make wine for medical and religious purposes – specifically communion wine. Charles Krug, Freemark Abbey, Louis Martini and the Beringers quickly got into the sacramental wine business. Households were still allowed to make up to 200 gallons of wine a year for home consumption, so enterprising people shipped grapes across the country for home winemakers. That business brought an industrious Italian immigrant family named Mondavi to California.

By the time Prohibition ended on 5 December 1933, only about a dozen Napa Valley wineries were still operating. Many talented winemakers, along with distillers and bartenders, had left the United States.

Though this was a dismal era for wine, there were also

positive developments. A new generation of pioneers started laying the foundation for the modern era of Napa Valley. John Daniel Jr, great-nephew of Gustave Niebaum, revived the legendary Inglenook, making wines that collectors still covet today. Louis Martini founded his winery before Prohibition ended, and was ready to sell wine the day the act was repealed. Others, like Roy Raymond, went to work for the Beringers in 1937, married into the family, and eventually founded Rutherford's Raymond Vineyards in 1970.

One of Napa's Valley's most exciting new arrivals was the Russian emigré André Tchelistcheff, Beaulieu's chief winemaker from 1938 to 1973. Tchelistcheff had fled the Russian Revolution as a teenager and fought with the White Army in the civil war; he studied oenology, first in Czechoslovakia and then France, where he met Georges de Latour, who persuaded him to come to Napa Valley. He would go on to become one of the most innovative and influential winemakers in Napa history; known as 'The Maestro', his legacy resonates today.

In 1943, three San Franciscans who were tired of city life escaped to Napa Valley to make wine. Former ad man

André Tchelistcheff

Robert Mondavi c. 1967

Joe Heitz, 1961

Fred McCrea and his wife Eleanor bought an old goat farm on Spring Mountain and later turned it into a white-wine focused vineyard called Stony Hill Winery; sales executive Lee Stewart purchased an old Howell Mountain winery and vineyard he named Chateau Souverain; and a young Stanford University graduate named Robert Mondavi learned that the Charles Krug Winery was up for sale.

This singleminded young man and his brother Peter convinced their parents to buy the once-great winery in St Helena. Cesare and Rosa Mondavi had arrived in the USA from the Marche in Italy at the beginning of the century. By the 1930s the family was living in Lodi and shipping grapes and winemaking supplies to home winemakers across the USA. But they realized that the future of wine lay in the Napa Valley. They bought Krug and dreamed of seeing their sons Robert and Peter build a family wine business together.

The 1960s: Robert Mondavi and a new generation

The 1960s were a time of upheaval in the USA, when racial minorities and women demanded equal rights as Americans. And it was an especially vibrant time to be in the Napa Valley. A new generation of well-travelled entrepreneurs came to the valley to create wines like the ones they loved in Europe, and to raise their families in the country.

Joe Heitz, an Illinois farm boy who had dabbled in wine while in the army and later worked with Tchelistcheff, founded Heitz Cellar in 1961 with his wife Alice. Jack and Jamie Davies left Los Angeles and bought Jacob Schram's old estate on Diamond Mountain in 1962, renaming it Schramsberg. They wanted to make American *méthode champenoise* sparkling wine that could rival champagne. Pharmaceutical executive Al Brounstein and his wife Adele started Diamond Creek on Diamond Mountain in 1968. And after making a fortune from hot coffee vending machines, Donn Chappellet and his wife Molly purchased 259 acres on Pritchard Hill, releasing their first wine in 1969.

The whole valley was abuzz when Robert Mondavi announced that he was starting his own winery. He had been feeling stifled at Charles Krug for a while because his family was reluctant to start ageing wine in expensive French oak as the best wineries in Europe did. Resentments grew, and a family dinner descended into insults and a fist-fight with his brother Peter.

When Robert was suspended from his family business, he saw it as an opportunity. He and his wife Marge found a site in Oakville, next to the Mondavi family's section of the To Kalon vineyard. They established a new winery in 1966, hiring architect Cliff May to design the classic adobe building with its distinctive arch that is an icon of Napa Valley. Robert Mondavi imagined it as a place where he could make elegant and ageworthy wines like ones he'd tasted at the great Bordeaux properties.

Mike Grgich

He hired the best talent, including Mike Grgich, who had escaped communism in Czechoslovakia with the dream of making wine

The To Kalon vineyard with Robert Mondavi Winery behind

in California, and Warren Winiarski, a Chicago philosophy professor-turned-winemaker.

As Zelma Long, Mondavi's winemaker from 1970 to 1979, notes, Napa Valley's wine industry was still in a nascent stage in that era. Wine was just another agricultural product, like walnuts and prunes. People grew grapes and made them into straightforward wine, often sold in large jugs meant for easy drinking.

'At the time I started in Napa, the wineries that were producing good wine were Beaulieu, Souverain and Inglenook,' Long recalls. 'And then Mondavi started in '66 and he was focused on stylistically more balanced, elegant styles of wine.'

Napa Valley wines were about to get a lot more attention, thanks to a marketing event at a wine shop in Paris.

The modern era: The Judgement of Paris

In 1976, Steven Spurrier, the proprietor of a small Paris wine shop called La Cave de la Madeleine, and his American business partner Patricia Gallagher, decided to host a tasting to celebrate the bicentennial year of the American

The Judgement of Paris: Patricia Gallagher, Steven Spurrier and the editor of *La Revue du vin de France*, Odette Kahn

Declaration of Independence. They thought it would be enlightening to pour the best California wines alongside top Bordeaux and Burgundy.

Spurrier secured the Californian wines with the help of tour guide Joanne DePuy, who was going to Paris with a group of vintners and negotiated with the airline to take them. 'Without Joanne, the wines wouldn't have got to Paris,' Spurrier said.

On July 4, nine eminent French journalists and critics gathered at the Intercontinental Hotel to blind taste and score a collection of ten red and ten white wines. The lineup of French wines included 1970 Château Haut-Brion, 1970 Château Mouton-Rothschild and 1973 Domaine Roulot Meursault 1er Cru Charmes. Everyone was shocked when the French critics gave the highest scores to two American wines: 1973 Stag's Leap Wine Cellars SLV Cabernet Sauvignon and 1973 Chateau Montelena Chardonnay.

The outcome might have gone unnoticed, but for an American journalist at the tasting. George M Taber, *Time* magazine's Paris correspondent, realised he had a big story when he saw the horror on the faces of the French panellists. The legend of the Judgement of Paris was born. The acclaim that it generated for the winning wineries in particular and for the Napa Valley in general forever changed the way the world looked at California's wine. It was clear that California had the terroir and the talent to produce wines on par with those from France, Italy, Spain and Germany. Warren Winiarski of Stag's Leap Wine Cellars and Mike Grgich of Chateau Montelena became famous overnight.

The 1980s and 1990s: Robert Parker ascendant

As wine became a more important part of the Napa Valley economy, in the 1980s winery owners and vineyard managers stopped simply farming grapes and focused even more on wine growing. By diligent work in the vineyard and winery, they aimed to rival and outdo the great wines of the world.

Wine critics and wine publications became more important in this period, and the most influential of all was a wine-loving lawyer named Robert M. Parker Jr, who launched *The Wine Advocate* in 1979. Parker's masterstroke was to invent the 100-point scoring system, by which

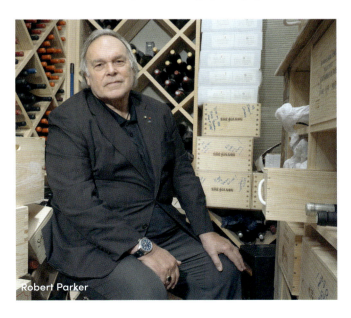
Robert Parker

Celebrated Napa Valley winemaker Heidi Barrett

any wine's (supposed) quality could be seen at a glance. Parker made his reputation as a wine sage after praising 1982 Bordeaux, a vintage that most of the wine world had dismissed as too ripe and not ageworthy, and which by the end of the decade was seen as one of the greatest of the century. He also was a big fan of the fruit-laden, higher-alcohol Cabernet Sauvignons that were starting to be released in Napa Valley. The 1985 Groth Reserve Cabernet Sauvignon was the first Napa wine that Parker awarded a perfect 100 points, and the entire valley and the wine community took note.

In the 1990s especially, Parker bestowed that perfect score on a string of Cabernet Sauvignon wines made by small, relatively unknown wineries tucked away in the hills above Oakville. In 1992, he awarded 100 points to the 1992 Dalla Valle Maya, as well as a new wine called Screaming Eagle. Both were made by Heidi Barrett, who became a sought-after international consultant. Other 'cult' wineries emerged: Harlan Estate, Colgin, Araujo, Pahlmeyer and Schrader, and Parker loved them all. High scores boosted sales and influenced other winemakers across the valley (and around the world) to make wines in a similar style.

Napa Valley's era of ripe and powerful Cabernets and Chardonnays reached its apotheosis (for some) with the 1997 vintage. A long, warm growing season produced grapes with record levels of sugar and many concluded the wines would be over-ripe, low in acidity and with no ageing potential. But the critics loved them, with more than one calling this the vintage of the century. A few holdouts still debate the ageworthiness of the '97s, but what is certain is that the huge success of the vintage ushered in a new era. 'Hang time' – leaving the grapes on the vine as long as possible – became the watchword. In many ways, it cemented Napa Valley's largely unfair reputation as a region producing only big, bold, ripe wines.

2000 and beyond

The 2000s were characterized by ripe and luscious – and very expensive - Cabernet Sauvignon blends by high-concept wineries like Hundred Acre, Scarecrow and others. By this time, though, there was also a loud backlash against the 'Parkerization' of wine, and calls for balanced wines that reflected terroir. Robert Parker retired in 2019 and today there's no one dominant wine critic.

One of the architects of the more balanced approach was Steve Matthiasson, a consultant in sustainable vineyard practice, who with his wife Jill, a botanist by training, now makes some of the most admired wines in the Valley. They

Sustainability advocates Steve and Jill Matthiasson

launched a wine brand in 2003 that focused on finding old vineyards and making terroir-driven, low intervention, higher-acid wines. That approach has influenced a whole generation of younger winemakers, who seek out forgotten Italian and French grape varieties of Napa's past.

The truth is that throughout the Valley's 'hedonistic' era, there were winemakers up and down the valley who never wavered from their desire to create wines that were balanced and restrained. From Cathy Corison, Cain Vineyard and Heitz Cellar, to less internationally known names like Snowden Vineyards, Spring Mountain's Stony Hill and White Rock Vineyards in Stags Leap District, some of the

The famous welcome sign outside Oakville has remained more or less unchanged since it was first put up in 1949.

Valley's residents have always made wines that evoke the finest styles of the 1970s.

Napa Valley's winemakers today are enjoying the freedom to make the style of wine that best represents their terroir; Americans are seeking out more food-friendly wines, with lower alcohol and brighter acidity. As tastes change, so the tide is turning: Cabernet Franc and Riesling are in the ascendant; you can find Albariño, Counoise, Chenin Blanc and Tempranillo on wine lists and on shelves. Cabernet Sauvignon still represents the majority of plantings, but Napa Valley in the modern era is more diverse in terms of grape varieties and styles than it has been for decades.

Geography

Even people who don't drink wine are drawn to the Napa Valley for its striking natural beauty. With the fog that hugs the hills in the early morning, the twin mountain ranges that border the valley and the distant peak of the volcano, Mount St Helena, it's one of the most memorable destinations in California.

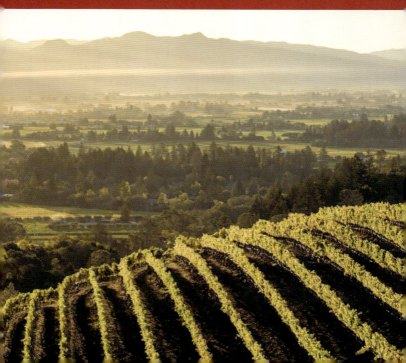

'Only five regions, or two per cent of the world's land mass, enjoy this type of weather'

Although we spend a lot of time in this book discussing the vineyards, grape varieties and top-flight growers, their work is profoundly shaped by the terroir, that wonderful combination of vine, soil, climate, topography and winemaker that creates a unique wine.

Napa Valley's volcanic and marine soils are among the most diverse and complex of any wine region. It has a Mediterranean climate characterized by warm and dry summers and mild, wet winters. Only five regions, or two per cent of the world's land mass, enjoy this type of weather: the Mediterranean Sea basin, South Africa, central Chile, south Australia – and California. All of these places are renowned for their wines. In Napa Valley, the balmy 21°C summers are getting hotter and dryer, with more frequent droughts and summer heatspikes, and increasing risk of devastating wildfires. Winters have become wetter, with heavy rains lasting days and occasional February snow that dusts the mountain tops. The Valley gets an average of 260 days of sunshine, which means grapes ripen fully and there are few problems with mould or mildew that can affect

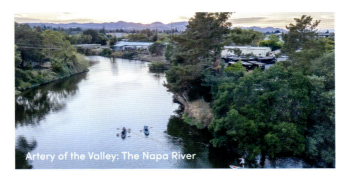
Artery of the Valley: The Napa River

The undulating landscape of northern Napa Valley in the fall

The extinct volcano Mount St Helena

European wine regions.

The Napa River, which meanders for 50 miles south from its source in St Helena, was once vital to commerce. Now it's a thriving – and strictly protected – recreational and wildlife habitat. The river feeds San Pablo Bay, north of San Francisco, which has a huge influence over the vineyards of Napa Valley, and Sonoma. The cool morning fog and chilly afternoon breezes from the Bay and the Pacific Ocean help create the important temperature difference between day and night – the diurnal shift – that makes the Napa Valley wines so distinctive. The greater the night-time drop in temperature, the easier it is for wine grapes to mature and ripen while retaining acidity, creating vibrant, balanced wines.

In terms of size, the Napa Valley wine region is relatively small, just 30 miles from north to south and five miles across from east to west at its widest point. Currently, the valley has a total of 45,342 acres (18,349 hectares) planted with grapevines. For context, Sonoma County next door has more than 60,000ha planted with vines while Bordeaux, 100,000ha, is many times bigger.

Situated on a fault line

The soil in Napa Valley is a mix of volcanic, alluvial and fluvial, reflecting geological shifts and changes that happened over millions of years. Geologists estimate that about 150 million years ago, tectonic plates shifted along the San Andreas fault and volcanoes erupted, giving birth to the twin mountain ranges that guard the valley: the Mayacamas and the Vacas. On the western side, the Mayacamas help shelter the Valley from rain and some effects of coastal fog, while the Vacas to the east offer shade from the intense afternoon sun and heat rolling in from the Central Valley.

The terrain was in flux, with mountain tops that slid from one site to another, and oceans and rivers that changed course, washing down sides of mountains depositing fossils, rocks and soil in v-shaped patterns known as alluvial fans. As the volcanoes erupted, they scattered soil and sedimentary rocks in all directions, leaving chunks of shiny obsidian glass and porous lava gravel rock across the valley.

The Valley itself formed about five million years ago and the result of all the geological tumult is the 33 soil series and more than 100 distinct types of soil found across Napa Valley's 17 sub-appellations or AVAs.

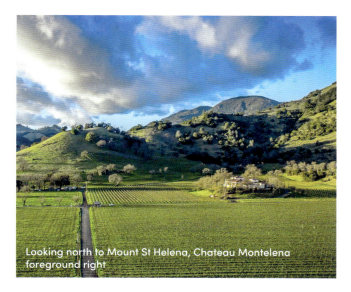

Looking north to Mount St Helena, Chateau Montelena foreground right

Napa Valley AVAs and their wines

American Viticultural Areas are to the United States what appellations of origin are to Europe: a guarantee that the wine in the bottle comes from a designated geographical area. But there are some crucial differences between an AVA and a French AOC.

Napa Valley wines started earning international acclaim at the end of the 19th century, but still the region didn't command much attention against the wines of Bordeaux, Burgundy and Germany, almost universally considered the best in the world. Throughout the first decades of the 20th century – for many reasons, among them the devastating effect of Prohibition (see p18) – Napa, and California, had little profile on the world stage. That situation began to change in the 1960s. Wineries like Beaulieu Vineyard, Heitz and Inglenook were already significant operations when Robert Mondavi opened his Oakville winery in 1966 and began to seriously market his wines around the world (see p21); then came the Judgement of Paris tasting in 1976, when Napa Valley Chardonnay and Cabernet Sauvignon bested the crème de la crème of French wine.

'The Valley started to be divided up into smaller sub-AVAs, as vintners and growers began to understand their land better'

A few years later, the Napa Valley brand was born: in 1981 the region was registered with the US federal government as an American Viticultural Area (AVA). It became a formidable marketing tool and soon after, the Valley started to be divided up into smaller sub-AVAs, as vintners and growers began to understand their land better and to work out which grape varieties grew best in which particular soils. They gave their regions individual identities to distinguish them from – and compare them to – the great wine regions of the world. So the different AVAs of the Napa Valley began to be registered.

The AVA System

As of 2024, Napa Valley AVA has 17 different sub-appellations. On paper, the boundaries of each sub-AVA are based on elevation and soil types. But in reality, politics plays a big role, with lines being drawn to deliberately include or exclude certain estates. There are a couple of important ways AVAs are different to European appellations. In the first place, they are dynamic: Napa Valley's latest is Crystal Springs AVA, incorporated in late 2024. Second, unlike in almost all European appellations, vintners have complete freedom as to which grapes they grow and how and when they plant and harvest them. To use an AVA name on the label, the regulations only require that 85% of the grapes in the bottle must come from that AVA.

Here's a quick guide to the 17 AVAs in Napa Valley from north to south, and some notable wineries found in each one. Although not an AVA, we have also included Pritchard Hill, which is an important and well-delineated hillside region on the eastern side of the Valley.

Calistoga

Even those who aren't into wine will have heard of the natural hot springs of Calistoga. The wines of this northernmost AVA are varied. They can be bold and higher in alcohol, but with careful picking decisions, the best offer balanced acidity. Established in 2009, Calistoga is the northernmost AVA and the hottest, since it's far from the

Calistoga

Diamond Mountain

bay's cooling breezes and ringed by mountains that hold in the heat. But cool air from the Pacific slips in at night, giving Calistoga vineyards the biggest diurnal shift: the difference between day and night temperatures can be as much as 10°C, which creates more complex and balanced wines. Of Calistoga's 12,703 acres (5,140ha), only 625 acres (252ha) are planted with vines. Elevation ranges from 300 to 1,200 feet (91 to 366m). Though the AVA includes mountains and flat areas, the soil is uniformly volcanic.
Notable wineries: Chateau Montelena, Frank Family Vineyards, Larkmead, Hourglass, La Sirena

Diamond Mountain District

Diamond Mountain District Cabernets are some of the most distinctive in the valley, powered by dark fruit, dusty cocoa and robust tannins. The Diamond Mountain District AVA was established in 2000, but winemaking dates back to the mid-1800s. Visionary Jacob Schram was the first to focus on planting hillside vineyards in 1862, like the ones from his home in Germany's Rheinhessen. Named for the obsidian glass that sparkles in the volcanic soil, Diamond Mountain is rocky, steep and difficult to farm, with elevations from 400 to 2,200 feet and just 500 acres (200ha) out of the available 5,000 acres (2,203ha) planted. Most wineries are small, the vineyards worked by hand; some of Napa Valley's most renowned wines are made here.
Notable wineries: Diamond Creek, Schramsberg, Theorem

Howell Mountain

Howell Mountain

Wines from Howell Mountain, part of the Vaca Mountain range in the north of Napa Valley, are known for dark fruit and firm tannins, and the potential for long ageing. Established in 1983, this was Napa Valley's first sub-AVA. The appellation mostly lies above the fog line rising from 1,400 to 2,600 feet (425 to 790m) in elevation, so western slopes enjoy ample afternoon sun. Just 1,500 acres (607ha) of the AVA's 14,000 acres (5,655ha) are planted with vines. Though the name suggests a peak, many Howell Mountain vineyards are planted on a plateau. Soils here are volcanic and well-drained.
Notable wineries: Dunn, Robert Craig, Cade

Chiles Valley District

Whether it's Zinfandel or Cabernet Franc, wines from this remote AVA in the Vaca Mountains tend to be balanced with nuance and complex flavours. Chiles Valley has a cooler climate and longer growing season, with most vineyards planted at 600 to 1,200 feet (180 to 365m) elevation. A dramatic landscape of twisted oaks and huge boulders, Chiles Valley was designated a sub-AVA in 1999 after a petition first filed by vintner Volker Eisele. The AVA is 6,000 acres (2,428ha), with 1,000 acres (405ha) under vine; the soils are a mix of volcanic areas with marine and alluvial silty clay on the valley floor. It is named after Joseph Chiles, a settler who received a Mexican land grant in 1841, and established a flour mill.

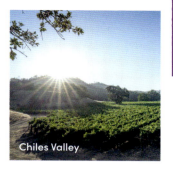
Chiles Valley

Notable wineries: Green & Red Vineyard, Brown Estate, Volker Eisele

Spring Mountain District

Spring Mountain is one of the highest and most beautiful of the mountain appellations. Cabernets from here tend to be a gentler expression of mountain wine, but wineries here specialize in everything from Cabernet Sauvignon to crisp Pinot Gris and aromatic Pinot Noir. The soils on these east-facing slopes of the Mayacamas range are varied – volcanic soils of the north and Franciscan sandy clay loam to the south – as are the microclimates, the vineyards tending to have numerous different aspects. The overall terrain is rocky with minimal well-drained soils, with 1,000

Sunset over Spring Mountain

acres (405ha) planted out of 8,600 acres (3,480ha). The elevations range from 600 to 2,600 feet (180 to 290m) and the climate is cooler than the valley floor, but the nights are warmer than in other mountain areas. The abundance of creeks and streams gave the mountain its name: it once supplied St Helena's drinking water. The historic Miravelle winery once made world-class wines here, a tradition carried on today by Spring Mountain's many small wineries. Spring Mountain was devastated by the Glass Fire in 2020: Newton's beautiful gardens were destroyed and the winery was subsequently closed. Cain lost 90% of its vineyard and its entire house and winery.
Notable wineries: Philip Togni, Fantesca, Stony Hill, Cain, Smith-Madrone

St Helena

St Helena is one of the sunniest and hottest areas in the valley, so there's no shortage of ripe full-bodied wines, as well as those with more finesse. The Napa Valley wine industry started in St Helena in 1861 when Charles Krug established his winery here; 20 years later there were over 100 wineries. Today, the town is a hub abounding with winemaking talent as well as some of the smartest hotels in the county, dozens of restaurants and some very famous wineries. An AVA since 1995, about a third of the 9,000 acres

St Helena

(3,640ha) in the St Helena AVA is planted with vines. Famous growing sites include the George Belden Crane, Capella and Madrona vineyards. Soils are a mix of volcanic soil to the north, turning to gravel and sandy soils along the benchland. The elevations range from 100 to 700 feet (91 to 213m).
Notable wineries: Corison, Heitz Cellar, Crocker & Starr, Spottswoode, Gallica, Snowden Vineyards

Crystal Springs

Though wine has been made here for generations, Crystal Springs is the newest AVA, incorporated in late 2024. The appellation sits between the St Helena, Calistoga and Howell Mountain AVAs, on the lower elevations of the Vaca mountain range. Wines from here can be aromatic with dark fruit notes

and quite brawny tannins that mellow over time. Elevations range from 400 to 1,400 feet (122 to 425m): crucially, most of the vineyards lie below the fog line, meaning cooler mornings and warm afternoons. It's a true mountain appellation with rocky slopes barely covered by topsoil, and many creeks and streams. Just 230 acres (93ha) of the available 4,000 acres (1,620ha) are under vine. Steven Burgess, former owner of Burgess Cellars, lobbied for the creation of the AVA.
Notable wineries: Viader, Somnium, Burgess

Rutherford

Rutherford occupies a special place in the hearts of those who love Napa Valley. Rutherford Cabernets have a youthful approachability and velvety tannins; the best share an indefinable quality known as 'Rutherford Dust,' an elusive combination of flavour and texture: stony minerality and fine-grained cocoa powder. Established in 1993, the AVA is named for Thomas Rutherford, who planted *vitis vinifera* vines on the 1,000 acres he received as a wedding present

in 1864. Inglenook and BV, the great pioneering estates that first made Rutherford Cabernet an object of desire, have been joined over the decades by other names of renown. The expansive AVA sees abundant sunshine, and has many microclimates and soil types. The most prized growing sites for Bordeaux varietals are along what is called benchland –the slopes which rise towards the foothills of the Mayacamas, where ancient rivers have left a mix of rocks and gravelly loam. The marine sand and clay mix on the valley floor is better suited to Sauvignon Blanc, Merlot and Chardonnay. Elevations range from sea level to 600 feet (182m) while 3,518 acres (1,425ha) of the AVA's 6,840 acres (2,768ha) are planted with vines.

Notable wineries: Inglenook, Tres Sabores, Alpha Omega, St-Supery, Frog's Leap, Quintessa, Staglin

Oakville

Oakville is a who's who of cult and household wineries making some of the most sought-after Cabernet Sauvignon in the world. Whether you prefer your Cabernet dark and concentrated or elegant and high-

toned, you'll find it here. Bounded by the Mayacamas on the west and the Vaca mountains to the east, sunlight and the right soils make Oakville one of the best places in the world for Cabernet Sauvignon. Its pedigree dates back to 1868, when HW Crabb dubbed his valley floor vineyard To Kalon, meaning 'the highest beauty' in Greek. His To Kalon wines won international awards, and generations later, Napa Valley titans including the Mondavi and Andy Beckstoffer battled over this hallowed site, known for its complex, dark fruited wines. Meanwhile, the mountains on the eastern side, home to Screaming Eagle, Tench Vineyard and Dalla Valle, produce brighter, red-fruited wines. Other acclaimed sites include Missouri Hopper and Martha's Vineyard. Groth Vineyards & Winery's 1985 Reserve Cabernet Sauvignon made history with the valley's first 100-point score from Robert Parker. An AVA since 1993, nearly every available bit of Oakville's 5,760 acres (308ha) is covered in grapevines.
Notable wineries: Screaming Eagle, Gamble Estates, Rudd, Dalla Valle, Harlan, Opus One, Far Niente

Atlas Peak

Another high, cool region, Atlas Peak makes Cabernet Sauvignon wines with intensity balanced by delicacy. It's still a largely underappreciated AVA – an inaccessible place of rugged beauty with bare, scrubby peaks and fields covered with giant boulders; there's ample grazing land for cows and few visitors. It's incredibly hard to farm such land, but its potential was recognised early on – wine has been made here since the 1870s. The landscape thrilled

Atlas Peak

Tuscany's Piero Antinori in the 1960s (he bought his estate in 1986): 'The arid landscape of rolling hills...the rocky soil ... the altitude and the cool breeze of the ocean reminded me of home,' he wrote. Winemaking here dates to the 1870s; the well-drained, red volcanic basalt soil is ideal for Bordeaux varietals. Established in 1992, the AVA is 11,000 acres (4,452ha) with about 2,000 acres (810ha) under vine, including part of the acclaimed Stagecoach Vineyard, one of the great Cabernet vineyards of Napa Valley whose winery clients are a roll-call of quality Napa Valley. Atlas Peak is distinguished by higher elevations from 760 to 2,600 (232 to 709m) with most vineyards around 1,400 feet (427m).
Notable wineries: Antinori Napa Valley, Stag's Ridge, Au Sommet

Stags Leap District

This small appellation, overlooked by the rocky outcrop called The Palisades, has a concentration of famous and pioneering wineries. The Cabernet Sauvignon that won the 1976 Judgement of Paris put Stag's Leap Wine Cellars (the eccentric apostrophes are the result of a drawn-out trademark battle) and this small, contained appellation on the international wine map. Winemaking here dates back to

Stags Leap District

the late 1870s; the original Stags Leap Winery was founded in 1893. Post-Prohibition, the area reverted to cattle country and fruit orchards, until the early 1960s, when a pioneering vintner called Nathan Fay planted Cabernet Sauvignon and made a wine that convinced Chicago philosophy professor Warren Winiarski to give up teaching and head west. After Winiarski's 1973 Stag's Leap Wine Cellars Cabernet won the Judgement of Paris (see p23), everybody wanted in. Three nearby property owners petitioned to be part of the AVA, and the federal government acquiesced. So what was originally a compact 500 acres (200ha) grew to a sprawling 2,700 acres (1,093ha) by the final approval in 1989. The eastern portion of the AVA is volcanic, but there are fluvial sections of clay and loam near the river, as well as sandstone and shale on the little hills that crop up throughout the AVA. Elevations here range from sea level to 500 feet (150m).
Notable wineries: Quixote, Stag's Leap Wine Cellars, Stags' Leap Winery, Shafer, Silverado, Cliff Lede, Chimney Rock

Yountville

The town of Yountville is named after George Yount, a midwestern farmer who left his family behind to seek fortune out West. He's considered the father of Napa Valley wine, since he was the first outsider to plant *vitis vinifera* vines and start a winery, around 1838.

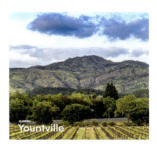

Though his early vinification methods were crude, one of his brightest moves was to hire the talented Charles Krug (see St Helena, above) as winemaker. The fledgling industry here was wiped out by phylloxera and Prohibition, and didn't really make a comeback until Domaine Chandon arrived in 1971. Though the town is tiny, the sprawling AVA, designated in 1999, encompasses more than 8,200 acres (3,320ha) of everything from volcanic soil with marine patches on the

Mount Veeder

east, rich fluvial soil in the center and sandy, gravel and clay loam in the west. The Sleeping Lady vineyard, noted for its elegance, is on the west side of town. And Yountville's little hills trap cool fog from the bay, making the AVA ideal for Chardonnay and Sauvignon Blanc as well as Cabernet.
Notable wineries: Chandon, Ad Vivum, Dominus

Mount Veeder

Bordeaux varietal wines from Mt Veeder are intense: deeply coloured, densely structured, richly flavoured, seamless and graceful in the right hands. Standing on a western slope of this ruggedly forested area, it feels like cold breezes from San Pablo Bay might blow right through you. An AVA since 1990, Mt Veeder takes its name from Peter Veeder, a minister and avid hiker from the Civil War era. The terrain is so rocky and steep that just 1,000 acres (405ha) of the 5,000 acres (2,025ha) in the Mt Veeder AVA are planted. Part of the Mayacamas range, vineyard elevations range from 500 to 2,600 feet (150 to 795m) – some of the highest in Napa Valley. The mountain soils are ancient seabed with shallow, well-drained soils that force grapevines to struggle,

producing small yields and tiny berries. Tannins can be ferocious up here – indeed, more than one veteran of these slopes calls Mt Veeder 'the Beast'.
Notable wineries: Mayacamas, Brandlin Estate, Pott Wines, Pym-Rae, Mt Brave

Oak Knoll District of Napa Valley

It's difficult to generalize about the taste of Oak Knoll wines. But given that this AVA established in 2004 is the coolest, foggiest and driest of all, wines tend to be expressive with balanced acidity. It's home to the most diverse range of grape varietals in Napa Valley, perhaps because settler Captain Joseph Osbourne ran a nursery that sold grapevine cuttings in the late 1800s. Soils are diverse too including volcanic soil to the east, clay and fluvial river deposits still fed by Dry Creek to the west. Elevations range from sea level to 800 feet (244m). More than half of Oak Knoll's 8,300 acres (3,360ha) are planted with grape vines, and wineries around the valley rely on Oak Knoll fruit.
Notable wineries: Matthiasson, Biale, Trefethen

Oak Knoll District of Napa Valley

Pritchard Hill

Even though it's not an official AVA, Pritchard Hill, which is known for red Bordeaux varietals, is considered the Rodeo Drive of Napa Valley because of its many iconic and exclusive wineries. A hilly fastness in the Vaca Mountains on the eastern side of the valley, most vineyards lie between 800 and 2,600 feet (244 and 793m). Charles Pritchard, a St Helena mayor, grew Riesling and Zinfandel here in the 1890s, and locals started to call his estate Pritchard Hill. Generations later, in 1967, after André Tchelistcheff advised them to plant mountain vineyards, Donn and Molly Chappellet purchased a property here; another early

Coombsville

Pritchard Hill

pioneer was the Long family, who first started buying land in the 1950s and founded David Arthur Vineyards in 1985. Over the decades they have been joined by some of the most renowned names in Napa, including Tim Mondavi (son of Robert) who sited his winery Continuum here. Most of the 1,300 acres (526 ha) of Stagecoach Vineyard (see Atlas Peak, earlier) are on Pritchard Hill. The soil is red volcanic clay loam known as Sobrante, and the landscape is littered with massive boulders.

Notable wineries: Bryant, Chappellet, Gandona, Continuum, Ovid, Colgin, Realm

Coombsville

Cognoscenti are calling Coombsville the next Oakville for the bright and supple but structured and ageworthy Cabernets that come from this cool region. Many wineries source their fruit from here. The relative proximity to San Pablo Bay gives Coombsville cooler conditions; in fact it was once a popular spot for Pinot Noir and Chardonnay. Named after Nathan Coombs, a pioneer and farmer who drew up the map for the town of Napa back in 1847, Coombsville became an AVA in 2011, though it's been planted with vineyards since the 1870s. The AVA is 11,000 acres (4,452ha) with

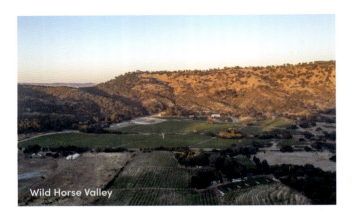
Wild Horse Valley

about 1,400 acres (567ha) under vine. Most vineyards are planted between 400 to 500 feet (122 to 152m) elevation, but some are as high as 1,000 feet (305m). The soils are mostly rocky and well-drained, ranging from volcanic ash to diatomaceous earth to reddish sediment from an ancient river.
Notable wineries: Caldwell, Shadybrook, J. Moss, Favia, Palmaz, Covert Estate

Wild Horse Valley

Wild Horse Valley is cooled by winds blowing in from San Pablo Bay, so it's ideal for Chardonnay and Pinot Noir, and the elevation gives the wines even higher acidity than Los Carneros. Grapes have been cultivated here since the late 1800s (the area is named for the wild horses that once lived there). An AVA since 1988, most of it is in Solano County, and it has few wineries. Though Kenzo Estate has 35 acres (14ha) of vineyards here growing Cabernet Franc, Sauvignon Blanc, Merlot and Malbec, the AVA name doesn't appear on their labels. An estimated 40 acres are planted in the area's reddish volcanic basalt soils; the vineyards lie at 840 to 2,130 feet (256 to 650m) elevation.

'The premier region for crisp sparkling wines, elegant Pinot Noir and Chardonnay'

Los Carneros

Los Carneros, which hugs San Pablo Bay, is the premier region for crisp sparkling wines, elegant Pinot Noir and Chardonnay (the best can reach the heights of Burgundy), and bright, lean Merlot. The Bay's influence means the vineyards are shrouded in morning fog and cooled with afternoon breezes, so grapes ripen slowly and retain acidity. Dating to 1983, Los Carneros was the first AVA to be defined by its climate and the only one that straddles both Napa Valley and Sonoma AVA. The soils of this 90-square-mile growing region are shallow sandy clay loam, while elevations range from sea level to 700 feet (213m). Los Carneros means 'the rams' in Spanish, and dates to the era when Mexico governed here. Wines from the Napa Valley side are labelled Los Carneros while those from Sonoma County are simply Carneros.

Notable wineries: Hyde Vineyard, Tres Perlas, Domaine Carneros, Ceja, Artesa, Bouchaine, Hudson

Los Carneros

The grapes

The Napa Valley has long been associated with two mainstay grapes: Chardonnay and Cabernet Sauvignon. It's odd if you think about it, since unlike European appellations, in which grape varieties are determined by law, in Napa Valley, potentially, anything goes: American AVAs do not dictate what kind of grapes can be planted.

That freedom was embraced in Napa Valley's early days, when in the 1960s Charles Krug Winery, the state's very first tasting room, poured wines made from 20 different varieties. Vintners liked experimenting and standing out from their neighbours — Joe Heitz made a unique Grignolino, a northern Italian grape, and Italian immigrants would plant many different varieties in one vineyard to make what was called a 'field blend'. The 1970 Napa County crop report shows farmers growing such obscure grapes as Sauvignon Vert and Golden Chasselas, Flora and Mataro.

But even then, Cabernet Sauvignon and Chardonnay were rapidly taking over. As Napa Valley's wine industry has matured, the acreage devoted to these grapes has increased exponentially. Making wine is expensive, so planting them makes financial sense, since they're the most popular wines in the USA.

Fortunately, there are still people in the Napa Valley who grow grapes and make wines for reasons that aren't purely driven by profit. There's beauty in growing what your grandparents grew, or in reviving a forgotten vineyard. And sometimes being an outlier is smart business: the rarity of both Cabernet Franc and Riesling means they both command a higher price per ton than Cabernet Sauvignon and Chardonnay.

Here's a snapshot on the currently reigning red and white grapes in the Napa Valley, and rising varietals to watch.

White Grapes

Chardonnay

Chardonnay can grow just about anywhere, but the best comes from the southern AVAs, which are cooled by breezes from San Francisco Bay. Napa Valley gained a reputation in the mid 1990s for big buttery Chardonnay; in the last decade or so, leaner, greener unoaked Chardonnay has emerged as a response (as did reds with a more nuanced oak profile). The best Napa Valley Chardonnays today offer a balance, with bright notes of citrus, golden apple, and stony minerality with hints of toast, vanilla, butter and hazelnut, depending on whether it went through full malolactic fermentation. and the degree of toast on the barrels used for ageing. It's tempting to describe as Burgundian the balanced Napa Valley Chardonnays from wineries including Hyde de Villaine, Antinori Napa Valley, Neyers, Trois Noix and Staglin, but they still have more fruit than an austere Chablis or a powerful Meursault.

Sauvignon Blanc

Though it's an afterthought in some regions, refreshing and fragrant Sauvignon Blanc is enjoying a renaissance in the Napa Valley. In the early days it became associated with inexpensive jug wines, but the grape's fortunes changed when Robert Mondavi renamed his wine Fumé Blanc, and aged it in oak, giving it more richness. Winemakers often add more layers to the wine by fermenting in different vessels including amphora, concrete egg, acacia wood and stainless steel and then blending the lots together. The aromatic Sauvignon Musque clone is often mixed in as well. Today, most Napa Valley Sauvignon Blancs are fresh with notes of pear, green apple, white flowers and minerals, though if the fruit is more ripe, it can show mango and roasted pineapple. Look out for Josephine Sauvignon Blanc from Turnbull Wine Cellars, Gamble Estate's Reserve wine, the ageworthy wines from Quintessa and Spottswoode and the luxurious Sauvignon Blancs from Vineyard 29, Futo Estate, Robert Mondavi I Block and Lail Vineyards' Georgia.

Sauvignon Blanc

Semillon

Laced with aromas and flavours of stone fruit, honey, lemon meringue and stones, Semillon is a relatively rare grape in Napa Valley, with just 56ha under cultivation. Though there's not much of it, Semillon is still an important grape for the texture and richness it can impart to leaner wines: it's a natural for blending with Sauvignon Blanc to make the classic white Bordeaux blends (Robert Mondavi Winery's Fumé Blanc is one excellent example). But Semillon can also shine in solo bottlings from The Vice and Matthiasson, as well as in late harvest wines like Dolce from Far Niente Wine Estates and Stony Hill's Semillon de Soleil.

Pinot Gris

Pinot Gris is known as Pinot Grigio in Italy and other European wine regions. The choice of name can indicate a different style of wine. Pinot Gris tends to be made in a richer style with oak treatment that brings out notes of white peach, melon, honey and lemon pith. Meanwhile, Pinot Grigio is usually made in a bright and lean Italian style with citrussy notes of lemony, green pear and green apple. Though just 31ha are grown here in the Napa Valley, you'll find both styles of wine. Hess-Persson and Sterling both make fine Pinot Gris, while Benessere, Laird Family and Housley Napa Valley bottle Napa Valley Pinot Grigio.

Viognier

Viognier is a grape that appeals to vintners who want to offer a rich, luscious wine that's a departure from the norm. The grape originates in the Rhône Valley of France and is made into weighty almost unctuous wines, most famously in Condrieu. Viognier in Napa Valley is made in a range of styles, from more lean and savoury (similar to a Chardonnay) to more lush with notes of mango, peach and white flowers. About 35.5 hectares of Viognier are being cultivated in the Napa Valley. Darioush, Freemark Abbey, Hyde, Stags' Leap Winery and Pride Mountain all make interesting Viogniers.

Red Grapes

Cabernet Sauvignon

In Napa Valley, there's no question that Cabernet Sauvignon is king. It's the most widely planted grape, with over 10,000ha under vine. Cabernet is also the most popular red wine in the USA, which explains why nearly every winery in the valley makes one. While Napa Valley gained a reputation for high alcohol, ripe and powerfully oaked Cabernet Sauvignon in the 1990s and early 2000s, that era has receded. You can still find big Cabernets, but most top estates are leaning into the balanced style pioneered by Robert Mondavi in the 1970s. There are many wonderful examples: seek out wines from Gandona, Diamond Creek, Heitz, Pott Wines, Paul Hobbs, Hourglass, Burgess, Stag's Leap Wine Cellars, Shafer, Realm, Silver Oak, Promontory, Mascot, Mt Brave and Jarvis.

Pinot Noir

You'll find pockets of Pinot Noir planted in the northern part of the Napa Valley, but almost all of the wineries which make Pinot are relying on vineyards in the cooler regions such as Los Carneros and Coombsville. New World Pinot Noir can range from delicate and floral, to bold in warmer areas. Napa Valley Pinot Noir wines from cooler areas often show notes of red plum, red raspberry and strawberry with hints of rose petals. In warmer areas, Pinot shows darker berries, black plum, bacon, cola and mushrooms. There are currently 991ha of Pinot Noir being cultivated in Napa County; notable producers are Hudson, Hyde, Hyde de Villaine, Bouchaine, Markham, Mi Sueño and Ceja.

Cabernet Franc

This classic variety from the Loire Valley and Bordeaux is becoming increasingly popular amongst Napa Valley winemakers. It has a more elevated aromatic profile than Cabernet Sauvignon and leans more towards freshness, red

Cabernet Sauvignon

fruits and spice. Expect hints of strawberry, raspberry, red plum and more unusual Chinese red fruit like schisandra or goji berry, accented by a hint of green peppercorn along with black tea and incense. With just 509ha under cultivation, it's in high demand, fetching more per kilo than Cabernet Sauvignon as more wineries appreciate it. Look for wines by Favia, Tres Sabores, Gamling & McDuck, Lang & Reed, Pott Wine, Brandlin Estate, Futo, Detert, Young Inglewood, Kenzo, Turnbull and Caldwell.

Zinfandel

While Cabernet Sauvignon is the main draw, Zinfandel is actually a very historic and important grape. This is a distinctly American varietal – no other country makes a wine called Zinfandel, though it's genetically identical to the Croatian Crljenak Kaštelanski and Italy's Primitivo. But since the mid 1800s, when Zinfandel arrived, it's been a mainstay in the local wine industry. During the mid 1970s,

The preservation of old vines is increasingly important

growing Zinfandel for white Zin allowed many family farms to stay afloat. Today, the 514ha of Zinfandel in Napa County are made into a range of styles including single-varietal wines, blends and ports. Zinfandel has a reputation for making powerful, high-alcohol wines, but the best are bright, balanced and food-friendly. Look out for wines from Tres Sabores, Biale, Ballentine, Frog's Leap, Brown Estate, Green & Red Vineyards, Turley and Frank Family.

Merlot

Merlot, the third most-planted grape in Napa Valley, is made into single varietal wines, or used in blends with Cabernet Sauvignon and other Bordeaux varietals to add plushness and fruit. Early ripening, with dark cherry, ripe berries, cocoa and plum flavours, Merlot is useful for softening the edges of Cabernet Sauvignon and is a sought-after blending grape. In fact, in the mid 1990s, Merlot fetched a higher price per ton than Cabernet. Today, you'll find it in a range of styles, from bold and structured (similar to Cabernet Sauvignon), to juicy and full of ripe fruit. Standout Merlots in the Napa Valley include the Duckhorn Three Palms bottling and Flint Knoll's Noble Right. In recent years, producers including Sullivan Estate, Blackbird, Markham and Mayacams are showing the more elegant side of Merlot by making wines with a higher acid profile.

Malbec

Malbec is originally from the Cahors region of southwestern France, where it has been grown for millennia and produces the region's famous deeply coloured 'Black Wines'. One of the classic five Bordeaux grapes, Malbec grown in the Napa Valley shows red and black fruit flavours of blackberry, plum and dark cherry with hints of violets and cocoa. There are 240ha planted in across the Valley. Although Malbec, like Merlot, is a popular blending grape, you'll also find delicious single varietal wines. Merryvale makes an excellent 100% Malbec; also worth noting are the Malbecs from Mi Sueño and Freemark Abbey.

Petite Sirah

Petite Sirah makes intense, deep purple wines with flavours of crushed purple berries, violets and often bold tannins. A cross between Syrah and Peloursin, it was originally called Durif after the French botanist who first bred the grape at his nursery in Tulles, France. Charles McIver brought it to the USA in the 1880s, and renamed it Petite Sirah. In Napa Valley's early days, Petite Sirah was often used as a blending grape to add depth and color to other wines. One of Napa Valley's most renowned Petite Sirah producers is Stags' Leap Winery (not to be confused with Stag's Leap Wine Cellars); also look out for wines from Green & Red, Biale, Brown Estate, Tres Sabores, Markham and Quixote.

Petite Sirah

10 historic Napa Valley wines

The 10 wines listed here are by no means easy to come by, but they do come up occasionally. If you get a chance to taste old Napa, take it – you'll be amazed by the balance, delicacy and precision of these venerable wines, some of which have passed into vinous legend.

There have been many legendary wines produced in Napa Valley over the decades. They were often made in small quantities, and winery economics dictated they should be quickly sold; today they live in private cellars, or collections like the David and Judy Breitstein Collection of historic wines at Napa's Culinary Institute of America at Copia – or only in memory. The best places to look are in shops like Acme Fine Wines (see **Napa Valley wine shops p158**) and online investment and auction sites such as Vinovest, Cult Wines and Wine Bid. We asked people who tasted these legendary wines to share their notes:

Inglenook Cabernet Sauvignon, Napa Valley 1941

The 1941 was dubbed 'the Napa Valley wine of the century' by James Laube of Wine Spectator. 'It was elegant with beautiful balance and integration. It was one of the great growths of Napa Valley at the time – the closest to Lafite,' says Robin Lail, daughter of John Daniel Jr who took over the legendary Inglenook in 1936. A bottle sold for $11,400 at Christies in 2011; another went for close to $25,000 in 2017.

Chappellet Cabernet Sauvignon, Napa Valley 1969

Philip Togni (who went on to open his own winery on Spring Mountain) and Donn Chappellet worked together on the inaugural 1969 vintage from the Pritchard Hill winery. 'Those were fairly young vines: dark fruited, spicy, structured,' says Phillip Corallo-Titus, Chappellet's current winemaker. 'It's considered one of the best wines ever made in California. It was recognized when it was young, and it has aged so beautifully and gracefully that now, 50 years on, it defies gravity.' In 2024 a five-litre bottle of the 1969 fetched $64,575 at auction.

Louis Martini Private Reserve California Mountain Barbera 1970

This wine, a great example of the Italian heritage of the Napa Valley, shows how wine was made in a bygone era. Spencer Graham, co-founder of Elizabeth Spencer Winery with his partner Elizabeth Pressler, opened a bottle for a tasting with the author in 2024. The wine was medium brick-red with a nose of malt, cola and sherry notes giving way to fig and plum. 'Silky and fine…mature now but holding very well' was *Decanter* magazine's verdict at around the same time. The bottle says 12.5% alcohol. As much as half of this wine, made by Mike Martini, was probably Petite Sirah.

Stag's Leap Wine Cellars SLV Cabernet Sauvignon, Napa Valley 1973

The winning Cabernet at the 1976 Judgement of Paris (see p23), the 1973 deserves its place in Washington DC's National Museum of American History. Marcus Notaro, Stag's Leap Wine Cellars director of winemaking, last tasted the wine in 2023. 'Upon opening and pouring the wine, it has aromas of tobacco, currants, and mocha along with some floral and cedar spice notes. It has a silky smooth texture, brick colour, with a long lasting finish and a touch of brightness. The taste and texture are the most exciting part … it truly shows the potential age-worthiness of the vineyard,' he noted. A bottle fetched $12,000 at auction in 2022.

Chateau Montelena Chardonnay, Napa Valley 1973

Montelena CEO Bo Barrett, who was just 20 when his father Jim sent their 1973 Chardonnay to Paris for Steven Spurrier's tasting (see p23), told *Decanter*, 'This is a classic house. We haven't gone from my father's original vision which is traditional styling with California flavours. By "traditional" I mean the European style – which has basically higher acid. All of our wines have a European model that they emulate. The reason it won the Paris Tasting is because it worked. It's supposed to taste like a white Burgundy and it still does.'

A bottle sold for $11,325 at Spectrum Wine Auctions in 2010.

Heitz Cellar Martha's Vineyard Cabernet Sauvignon, Oakville 1974

Widely considered one of the best early Heitz vintages and much sought-after by collectors.

'The 74 is really legendary,' Carlton McCoy, CEO of Lawrence Wine Estates (owner of Heitz Cellar), says. 'It's a knockout wine, one of the great wines of the region.' In August 1994 Robert Parker noted, 'The spectacular, huge, Mouton-Rothschild-like nose of mint, cassis, lead pencil and toast is remarkably youthful. Staggeringly concentrated, this full-bodied, super-rich wine possesses moderate tannin, fresh, lively acidity and a blockbuster, rich, fleshy finish. This is a monumental effort!'

In 2021 a magnum of the 1974 sold at Sotheby's New York for $5,500.

Robert Mondavi Winery Cabernet Sauvignon, Napa Valley 1974

The older vintages from Mondavi are among the most sought-after Napa Valley Cabernets – the 1974 was the favourite vintage of Zelma Long, Mondavi winemaker from 1970-1979. 'Mondavi drove the style to more elegance,' she says. 'Seventy-four was a great wine, beautiful and flavourful. It was a good season. It was all the things you like: sunny, not rainy at critical times, not excessively hot. The grapes had time to ripen before harvest. They were relatively high

in sugar compared to the other years, but they were still in the 12% range.' It's also affordable and relatively accessible, with bottles going for around $300.

Caymus Cabernet Sauvignon Grace Family Vineyards, Napa Valley 1978

It's called Napa Valley's first cult wine, especially since Dick Grace sold his 50 cases for $25 a bottle to both retailers and consumers, an astronomical amount at the time. 'The thing that caught everybody's attention was the balance of the wine,' Grace says. They had grafted on Bosché clone vines from Freemark Abbey as a hobby (although care was taken over planting density and keeping the plot organic), and driven the 1978 harvest over to Caymus Winery to vinify them. When Charlie Wagner, who ran Caymus, sampled the grapes, he said, 'You know, Dick, this is damned fine fruit.' They bottled it separately, and the Grace Family Vineyards label was born.

The wine rarely comes up for auction but most recent data suggests around $600 per bottle is the average price.

Dalla Valle Maya Proprietary Red Blend, Napa Valley 1992

This was the first 100-point wine for the winery founded by Naoko and Gustav Dalla Valle in the eastern hillsides of Oakville in 1986. Today the winery is run by Naoko and her daughter Maya. 'The 1992 growing season, while not heralded as a great year in the valley, was perfect for our site,' Maya says. Robert Parker agreed. 'This wine [a Cabernet Sauvignon-Cabernet Franc blend made by Heidi Barrett]... possesses great fruit, superb density, wonderful purity and balance, and a compelling extra dimension both aromatically and texturally. Destined to be a legendary wine,' the critic noted, giving it 100 points. Available for $845 from cultwine.com.

Screaming Eagle Cabernet Sauvignon, Oakville, 1992

The first vintage from one of California's – the world's – most famous wineries. What founder Jean Phillips called 'my beautiful ranch with my precious little winery', Screaming Eagle has been making headlines for decades. The wines are rare (fewer than 500 cases of the 92 were made) and command serious prices (a bottle of the 2013 is on the list at London's Hedonism for £3,750). Winemaker Heidi Barrett recalls 1992 'was a remarkable weather year, grapes were delicious across the board and there was also a bigger crop. It's not unlike what I do now, with that same purity of fruit. Robert Parker mentioned pure dark cherry cassis flavors. It was a very balanced, complete wine.' Parker rated it 100 points.

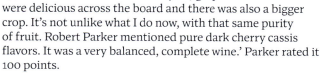

A bottle of the 1992 sold for $10,000 at auction at Christie's in 2022.

The Judgement of Paris, 1976. Steven Spurrier foreground

Towns of Napa Valley

From the busy streets of the capital to the well-heeled chic of St Helena, Napa Valley's towns are all very different. Here's a quick guide to what to expect from each.

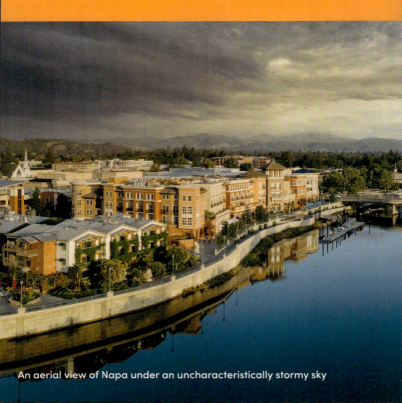

An aerial view of Napa under an uncharacteristically stormy sky

Napa's historic riverfront and Third Street Bridge

Napa

Just an hour north of San Francisco, the county seat of Napa County is the most vibrant of the towns that make up the Napa Valley. Whether you want to shop, sip wine, see a show or sleep, you can do it all here. The Napa River made the young city a hub for commerce, and today there's a promenade along the river as well as historic buildings filled with popular restaurants, inns and bars. The Napa County Airport is a convenient landing point for jetsetters who want to fly private.

The downtown area is home to more than 60 tasting rooms including The River Club, Benevolent Neglect, No Love Lost, Downtown Brown and Gamling & McDuck. Favourite restaurants include Winston's for breakfast and lunch, Lil Sista's Goodys for southern fare, Stateline Road for midwestern barbecue, Tarla for Mediterranean small plates and Croccante Pizza for excellent pies including a gluten-free Detroit-style pizza.

Don't miss exploring the Oxbow Market, a food hall with excellent choices including Ritual Coffee, Oxbow Cheese & Wine Merchant, Hog Island Oysters, gourmet market Hudson Greens & Goods and The Fatted Calf for house-made charcuterie and exquisite meat. If you have

Eagle Vines Golf Course, American Canyon

extra time and want to get outdoors, make the hour drive out to Lake Berryessa, the largest lake in the region. In warm weather, it's a popular spot for fishing, hiking and camping.

American Canyon

American Canyon is just under an hour's drive from San Francisco, about 20 minutes from downtown Napa City and about 40 minutes to St Helena. For most visitors it's a stop on the way to wine country, perhaps to fill up with petrol or grab a cup of coffee. Predominantly a bedroom community with many homes and apartments, takeout restaurants and grocery stores, it's good for essentials like groceries to stock a rental house; if you don't mind driving a bit to get to the heart of Napa Valley, it's worth considering as a base for your wine trip: there are inexpensive chain hotels, trails for hiking and running, including American Wetlands Trail and Newell Open Space Preserve, as well as the 18-hole Eagle Vines Golf Course.

Yountville

A town of only 3,300 residents, thousands more flock to Yountville for the combination of fine dining, luxury spa resorts and wineries. A major draw for many is Thomas Keller's three Michelin-starred French Laundry (Keller runs four other establishments in Yountville, including the popular Bouchon Bistro and Bouchon Bakery).

Yountville, named for early white settler George Yount, dates to the 1850s, but the town wasn't legally established as a municipality until 1965. About an hour and a quarter's drive minutes from San Francisco, it's well situated for travellers who want to visit wineries in both the northern and southern parts of the Napa Valley. It's an easily walkable town with sculptures and statues along the meandering sidewalk. Yountville is also home to the Napa Valley Museum, which mounts exhibitions that explore fine arts and Napa Valley history. High-end stays include Bardessono, Estate Yountville, Maison Fleurie and North Block Hotel & Spa. Domaine Chandon is still a must-visit, and other

Downtown Yountville

wineries include Hill Family, JCB Tasting Salon and Cliff Lede. Everyday dining options include R+D Kitchen, ad hoc, Bouchon and RH.

St Helena

St Helena is home to some of the valley's oldest wineries, including Charles Krug and Beringer. This small city is undeniably the hub for the crème de la crème of the wine industry: the people who grow the finest grapes, own wineries or design them. It's a cute place to walk around and look at the historic homes and churches, shop along Main Street or settle in for a picnic or summer concert at Lyman Park. And it boasts a concentration of casual and fine restaurants: the excellent Press and its new venture Understudy (an upscale food market or 'culinary playground'), Farmstead, The Charter Oak and Tra Vigne. In the centre are Goose & Gander, Cook and Charlie's, and Brasswood Bar & Kitchen at the north end of town. Shop at the well-stocked Sunshine Grocery for provisions, grab legendary English muffins from the original Model Bakery or pick up a sandwich from Giugni's (pronounced Joo-nee's) deli, a burrito from Azteca or a quick meal from Gott's Roadside

High street, St Helena in the fall

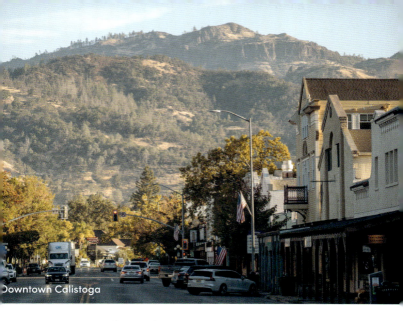

Downtown Calistoga

or Station St Helena. When the game is on or you feel like drinking beer, head to Ana's Cantina. St Helena is about 90 minutes north of San Francisco, and a good 30 minutes from Napa though the drive takes longer during rush hour.

Calistoga

The name Calistoga is synonymous with wellness thanks to its natural mineral hot springs and healing mud. San Francisco entrepreneur Sam Brannan built a hotel there (guests can still stay in one of the historic cottages) and established the town in 1867. A big part of Brannan's success was getting a railroad installed to bring visitors from San Francisco to Calistoga. It's the northernmost town in the Napa Valley, and it takes an hour and 45 minutes to drive from San Francisco to Calistoga. The city offers a mix of wineries including Chateau Montelena, Frank Family Vineyards, Hourglass, Larkmead, Sterling Vineyards with its tram, sparkling wine house Schramsberg, Lola Wines and

Two well-known, if rather touristy, Calistoga attractions are the Castello di Amorosa (above) and the Old Faithful geyser (right). The Castello is a strictly 20th century affair, built by winery owner Dario Suttui in the late 1990s at a cost of some $40 million using old-world materials and construction techniques. The Old Faithful geyser (not to be confused with its bigger counterpart in Yellowstone National Park) lets off volcanic steam at regular 15-30 minute intervals.

Tank Garage Winery in a historic petrol station. Calistoga has a vibrant, slightly funky and walkable downtown area with a mix of restaurants, hotels, small shops, wine tasting rooms and cocktail bars. The range of places to stay include The Four Seasons and Solage as well as smaller hot springs inns and B&Bs. For dining, local favourites include Robert's Tropical Table for cocktails and tasty appetizers; Sam's Social Club for seasonal fare and drinks; Lovina, which does American farm-to-table fare with gluten-free options; and Creole-Cajun Evangeline run by a Michelin-starred chef. Head to Cal-Mart for cheese, soft drinks and provisions. Don't miss stopping by The Depot, Jean Charles Boisset's multi-use space with cafe, wine and spirit tasting, souvenir shop and museum dedicated to Brannan.

Experience a taste of the good life in Napa Valley

The best things in life are the experiences we share, savour, and discover. Nowhere is that more apparent than in Napa Valley, where anyone – and everyone – can experience a taste of the good life.

Napa Valley sets a global standard for exceptional experiences – the perfect blend of world-class wineries, renowned dining experiences, industry-leading amenities, outdoor adventure and serene surroundings. As Napa Valley's official ambassadors, the team at Visit Napa Valley works to ensure that every visitor experiences a taste of the good life – and all our premier wine country destination has to offer.

Napa Valley comprises five unique and distinctive towns: American Canyon, the City of Napa, Yountville, St. Helena and Calistoga. The compact geography of the valley, at 35 miles (56km) long by five miles (8km) wide, means it's easy to discover each town. Visitors can enjoy breakfast in American Canyon, taste wine in Yountville, shop in St. Helena, relax at a spa in Calistoga and be back in time for dinner in the City of Napa—all in one day. No two Napa Valley towns are alike – they each make for a remarkable Napa Valley blend.

With over 400+ wineries open to the public, Napa Valley offers unparalleled wine experiences throughout the region, and renowned

ways to unwind. In addition to its famed wine country heritage, Napa Valley is one of the premier wellness destinations in the United States. Each year, visitors flock to the region to 'take the waters' and enjoy natural geothermal springs and world-class wellness experiences, from mud treatments to massages to sound baths.

Trailblazing eco initiatives are the cornerstone of the Napa Valley ethos. We take pride in the beauty of the natural setting and understand our role in protecting and preserving Napa Valley for generations to come. Our wineries, restaurants, and hotels within the valley have prioritized sustainable and eco-friendly practices, having embraced conservation and land stewardship for many generations. There are more than 90 Napa Green Certified Wineries, and the Napa Valley is home to 40% of all certified sustainable wineries in California. The majority of our hotels and resorts are committed to sustainability, water conservation and green housekeeping practices.

Everyone is welcome in Napa Valley. We champion diversity, equity, inclusivity and accessibility, and demonstrate and foster a creative spirit, welcoming artists, creators and craftspeople of all backgrounds, while ensuring resident quality of life and the protection of our natural resources.

Go to **VisitNapaValley.com** for official visitor resources, including trip inspiration, itineraries, digital tools and guides to plan an unforgettable stay.

Content supported by Visit Napa Valley

Visiting Napa Valley

Napa Valley is blessed with a climate that makes visiting in any season a pleasure. This section will help you plan your visit, whether you want to catch a festival or be here for harvest; wine routes and other attractions are included at the end of the section.

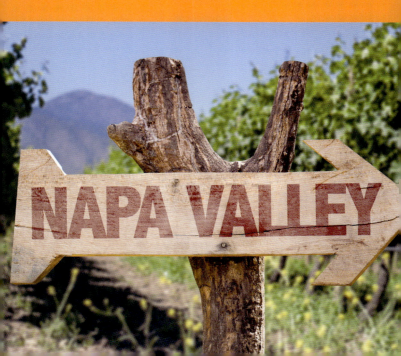

When to visit

Winter (December to February)

This is a quiet time in the valley. Though the grapevines are dormant and bare, plentiful winter rains ensure that everything remains green. The temperatures range from 4.4°C to 20.5°C. Wineries are busy with tasks like bottling, but there are fewer visitors so it's easier to make an appointment even at the last minute. The same is true for popular restaurants and hotels. Mustard flowers, planted to fix nitrogen in the vineyards, bloom a bright yellow in January and peak in mid-February.

Spring (March to May)

The pink buds on grapevines across the valley have usually sprouted tiny pale green leaves by now. Temperatures are consistently between 8.3°C to 20°C. This is a crucial time in the valley as growers pray that there are no freezing temperatures or hail to damage the delicate new shoots. It's a great time to visit, as it's the start of the outdoor season, but be sure to dress in layers and bring along your umbrella.

Summer (June to August)

Napa Valley is in full swing in summertime. It's sunny outside nearly every day with average temperatures of 15.5°C to 29°C. Everyone wants to be here during summertime, so you'll need to book wine tasting, hotel and restaurant reservations well in advance. Days can be intensely hot but even in high summer you'll want a jacket, jumper or wrap for the evenings as temperatures in the Valley drop considerably.

Autumn (September to November)

Autumn is a magical time to visit the Napa Valley. There's a hum of activity as harvest kicks off in earnest in September (the crush, as it's known, lasts from late August to early November). You'll be able to smell the fruity scent of grapes fermenting as you drive around the valley. Temperatures hover between 10°C to 25°C and it's a good time for festivals. Wineries see their peak visitors during autumn and traffic can be heavy.

Festivals

There are year-round festivals celebrating local wine, food and culture throughout Napa Valley. This is a selection – almost all have excellent and informative websites.

Napa Valley Restaurant Week (January)

This all-valley festival brings rolling dining discounts and specials to popular restaurants from one end of the valley to the other. Check the Visit Napa Valley website to learn more details.

visitnapavalley.com

Napa Truffle Festival (January)

Over this three-day festival, local and visiting chefs create black truffle delicacies paired with wines.

napatrufflefestival.com

Yountville International Short Film Festival (January)

More than 100 filmmakers from around the globe come to show their work in the heart of wine country, with screenings a short stroll away from restaurants, bars and at least 14 tasting rooms.

yisff.com

Napa Valley Mustard Celebration (January to March)

The yellow mustard that blooms in Napa Valley vineyards is a bright harbinger of spring. A series of art gallery showings and food events from January to March culminates in big party at CIA Copia on 29-30 March.

napavalleymustardcelebration.com

hot air balloon over yellow mustard field

Bottle Rock Napa Valley

Hall Winery Cabernet Cookoff (April)

A big tasting at the St Helena winery, with chef teams from all over the country competing to create a dish that goes best with the winery's Cabernet, to win funds for their favourite charity.

hallwines.com

Taste of Oakville (May)

Join wineries in this famed wine district for a walk-around tasting at Robert Mondavi Winery's Arch & Tower restaurant in downtown Napa.

tasteofoakville.ca

BottleRock Napa Valley (late May)

Wine and music converge at this homegrown festival at the Napa Valley Fairgrounds that draws major acts each year, from Stevie Nicks to Justin Timberlake to Public Enemy.

bottlerocknapavalley.com

La Onda (June)

One of the largest Latino music festivals in the USA, with bilingual performances in Spanish and English at Napa's Fairgrounds.

laondafest.com

Collective Napa Valley (June)

A star-studded charity wine auction, run by Napa Valley Vintners. This fundraiser features barrel tastings, gourmet cuisine, winery dinners and bidding on barrels of wine to support local community service organizations. One of the valley's most exciting weekends for wine lovers.

collectivenapavalley.org

Festival Napa Valley (July)

Festival Napa Valley brings world-class opera vocalists, musicians and dancers of every genre to the valley for ticketed performances spread over two weeks.

festivalnapavalley.org

Rutherford Chili Ball (August)

Put on your cowboy hat and boots and enjoy chilli paired with Rutherford wines in this long-running event.

rutherforddust.org

The Black Radio Experience (August)

Enjoy three days of live jazz, hip-hop, R&B performances plus DJ sets at this event hosted by Blue Note Jazz Festival at The Meritage Resort.

bluenotejazz.com/black-radio-experience

PGA Tour Procore Championship (September)

This tournament hosted at Silverado Resort every September kicks off the Professional Golf Association's autumn season. Purchase tickets to see the action or just enjoy spotting top golfers having dinner around the valley.

procorechampionship.com

Napa Lighted Art Festival

One Mind Music Festival for Brain Health (September)

Staglin Family Vineyard hosts an important and lavish event with a scientific symposium, celebrity chef dinner and concert (pictured: singer-songwriter Elle King in 2024). It raised more than $3million in 2024, the 30th anniversary of Garen and Shari Staglin's founding of the One Mind organisation.

onemind.org staglinfamily.com

Napaulée (November)

Napa Valley's end-of-harvest party. Inspired by La Paulée in Burgundy, Press restaurant in St Helena hosts this charity byob, with an indulgent menu, themed dress and an auction. Filled with winemakers and lots of folks who love to share wine and dance

pressnapavalley.com

Napaulée in St Helena

Napa Lighted Art Festival (December)

'A celebration of creative arts, technology and lights', this slightly nerdy but nevertheless dramatic festival brings lighted art installations and projected light designs to the streets of Napa.

donapa.com/lighted-art-festival

How to Get Around

Most Napa Valley visitors fly into one of three international airports: San Francisco (SFO), Oakland (OAK) or Sacramento (SMF); Napa County Airport (APC) does not have any commercial flights. The Napa Valley is about 50 minutes from Oakland, 1.5 hours from San Francisco, and about 65 minutes from Sacramento. San Francisco to St Helena in the centre of the valley takes at least two hours; at peak times traffic can be very heavy. Many visitors rent a car or hire a private driver to take them around in a limousine or sports utility vehicle. Larger groups may want to hire a tour shuttle bus to take them to wineries.

The Wine Train that runs from Napa to St Helena and back is a scenic way to enjoy valley views from the comfort of a restored vintage carriage. However, instead of a hop on, hop off train, The Wine Train offers set routes and packages. The three-hour package includes lunch, a tasting

Napa Valley Wine Train

at Grgich Hills, and a return trip to Napa for $325 to $385 per person. Guests can also enjoy lunch, dinner or special experiences like tea with Domaine Chandon wines for $225 to $325 per person.

The Napa Valley Transit Authority operates a public bus called The Vine that has set routes around the county. And guests can hire rideshare cars through Uber and Lyft.

Bike Tours

Touring the vineyards under your own steam or on an e-bike is convenient, healthy and far cheaper than hiring a limo. Many hotels offer rentals, and shops such as the **Calistoga Bike Shop** and **Napa Valley Bike Shop** in downtown Napa will deliver to your hotel. Several tour operators do bike tours – check out **Getaway Adventures** (getawayadventures.com) and the **Napa Valley Vine Trail** (vinetrail.org), a nonprofit dedicated to building a walking/biking trail system to connect the entire Napa Valley.

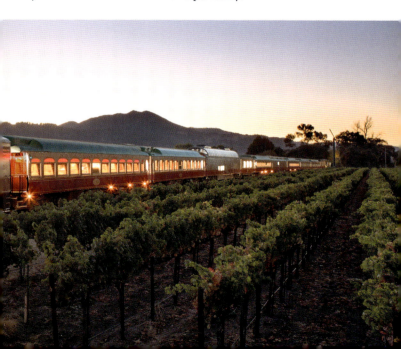

Louis M. Martini

One of Napa Valley's most historic wineries invites you to experience our storied past and look to our exciting future

The first Napa winery built after the repeal of Prohibition in 1933, Louis M. Martini was instrumental in re-establishing the valley and restoring its world-class reputation. The Martini family's renown as both community leaders and technical innovators is backed by a long list of accomplishments and their steadfast commitment to craftsmanship.

They were co-founders of the Napa Valley Vintners and early practitioners of ground-breaking techniques that have since become standard, including hillside planting of Cabernet Sauvignon, clonal selection, varietal labelling, reserve bottling, temperature-controlled fermentation, and more.

Today, Louis M. Martini continues to focus on small-lot production of Cabernet Sauvignon in their restored St Helena winery, welcoming new friends and seasoned collectors alike to taste some of Napa Valley's most celebrated wines.

Louis M. Martini is where Napa Valley's past, present and future can be seen, felt and tasted. Built in 1933 and restored in 2019 by famed architect Howard Backen, our winery honours our history and raises a toast to the next century.

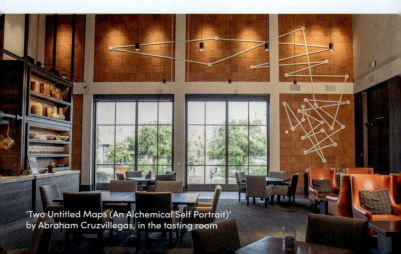

'Two Untitled Maps (An Alchemical Self Portrait)' by Abraham Cruzvillegas, in the tasting room

The Howard Backen-designed restored winery by night

In our iconic tasting room, the surrounding valley and working winery are part of the experience. Guests can peer into oak barrel cellars, where our wine is hand-crafted with the same care and attention to detail as it was nearly a century ago.

The winery is also home to an ever-increasing collection of art. Each year, a contemporary artist whose work explores the deeply intertwined themes of the world of art and the process of winemaking is invited to create a permanent, site-specific or site-responsive work for Louis M. Martini. These works delve into subjects such as the passage of time, the beauty of our environment, the richness of history and culture, and the nuances of sensory experience.

Our culinary team, led by Napa Valley native Chef Aaron Meneghelli, further enhances the guest experience with seasonally changing pairing menus that bring out the best in each vintage. With a variety of tasting experiences on offer, Louis M. Martini is a must-visit winery for a glimpse of Napa's storied past and a look at its exciting future.

Wine and food pairing in the Heritage Lounge

Please note: While walk-ins are welcome, it is best to book in advance.

Content supported by Louis M. Martini

Wine routes

Whether you're winding through mountaintop vineyards, exploring the estates that shaped Napa Valley's legacy or discovering the spots where locals gather, these itineraries show you the best tasting experiences, the most stunning scenery and the unforgettable meals. The wineries listed (unless otherwise stated) are open to visitors; almost all need to be pre-booked online. You will find more suggestions for wineries to visit and where to eat, drink and stay in The Guide (p122).

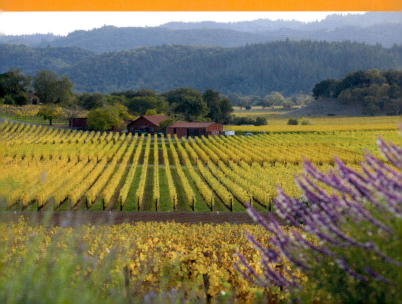

ITINERARY 1
Mountain Wineries

Making your way into Napa Valley's mountains is as thrilling as the wines themselves. The roads twist and climb through towering redwoods and dense conifer forests, offering glimpses of the valley below before opening to breathtaking vistas. As you ascend, the air grows cooler, the vineyards steeper and the sense of remoteness ever more pronounced. These elevations – perched along the **Vaca** and **Mayacamas mountain** ranges – are home to some of Napa Valley's greatest vineyards and wineries. Up here, time is of the essence—distances are deceptive, the roads are winding and reception is patchy so you can't rely on satnav. Plan your route, book in advance and ideally, hire a driver.

Pritchard Hill

A 30-minute drive from downtown Napa, **Continuum Estate** [1] crowns **Pritchard Hill**. It's one of the region's most spectacular panoramas: standing outside the winery, the valley sprawls beneath you, stretching from San Pablo Bay and the town of Napa to Calistoga and the distant peak of Mount St Helena. If your eye's keen you can spot **Vine Hill Ranch** [2], **To Kalon Vineyard** [3] and the back elevation of **Harlan's Promontory Estate** [4].

Pritchard Hill is also home to **Colgin Cellars** [5], where in addition to world-class Cabernet Sauvignon, they make one of Napa Valley's most Rhône-like Syrahs; **Chappellet** [6], a historic estate known for age-worthy, structured reds that exemplify mountain terroir.

Howell Mountain

A visit to Howell Mountain brings you into one of Napa Valley's most distinctive growing regions, where high elevations and volcanic soils create deeply structured, long-lived wines. At **CADE** Estate [7], expect precise, mountain-grown Cabernet Sauvignons farmed organically, with an elegant tension that balances richness with freshness. As

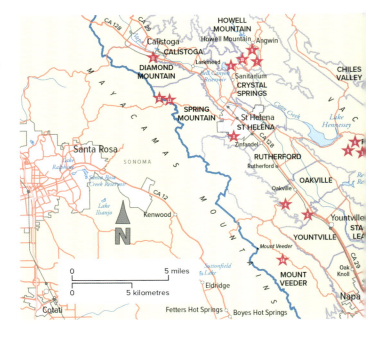

you ascend Deer Park Road, you'll pass through the newly designated **Crystal Springs AVA (see p43)**, home to **Burgess Cellars' Sorenson Vineyard [8]**. **Arkenstone [9]** is known for mineral-driven Sauvignon Blancs; further along, **Dunn Vineyards [10]** seems almost detached from Napa Valley, rooted in the clouds.

Diamond Mountain and Spring Mountain

At the northern reaches of Napa Valley, **Diamond Mountain** is home to one of the valley's most visually arresting vineyards: **Diamond Creek [11]**. A valley within a valley, this estate is defined by its dramatic terraces and rugged slopes.

Continuing south, **Pride Mountain Vineyards [12]** straddles the Napa-Sonoma county line, its cellar adorned with menus from the White House state dinners where its

wines have been poured. At **Vineyard 7&8 [13]**, former Harlan and Bond winemaker Wesley Steffens makes bold, lush Cabernet Sauvignons that echo the mountain's wild beauty. Topping the Mayacamas Range, **Mayacamas Vineyards [14]** is a piece of Napa Valley history. Its 1971 Cabernet Sauvignon was a contender in the 1976 Judgement of Paris tasting, cementing its place among the valley's legends. Today, the winery remains a standard-bearer for old-school, structured, long-lived Napa Valley Cabernets.

Where to Eat

Calistoga With so much tasting, a well-planned meal strategy is essential. If time is tight, grab a gourmet sandwich at **Cal-Mart** in Calistoga, or try **House of Better**, a wellness-focused restaurant that blends Mexican and Californian flavours.

St Helena For a more leisurely lunch, book a table at **Charlie's** in St. Helena, where ex-French Laundry veteran Elliot Bell's fried chicken is legendary, or head to **The Station**, run by Joel Gott of Gott's Roadside, for healthy salads, cold-pressed juices, espresso and an unforgettable chocolate chip cookie.

Yountville Go all-in on indulgence at **Bouchon** with Champagne, oysters and profiteroles.

The view from Myacamas Vineyards

ITINERARY 2
The Valley Floor

If you're staying in Napa City, a visit to **Hyde de Villaine (HdV)** [1] in Trancas St is essential. This collaboration between the Hyde family (Napa Valley) and the de Villaine family (of Burgundy's Domaine de la Romanée-Conti) produces Chardonnays and Merlots of stunning balance, restraint and ageability.

From there, head up the Silverado Trail and take a right up Soda Canyon Rd, where you will find **The Caves at Soda Canyon** [2], a boutique collective high in the hills where a tasting of Okapi Wines unfolds deep within the cave system.

The **Rutherford** appellation, north of Yountville and south of St Helena, offers an array of experiences. If you're looking for something off the beaten path, **The Terraces** [3] has an unforgettable **all-terrain vehicle tour** through vineyards and orchards and wild terrain, followed by a seated tasting of their small-production wines.

Inglenook

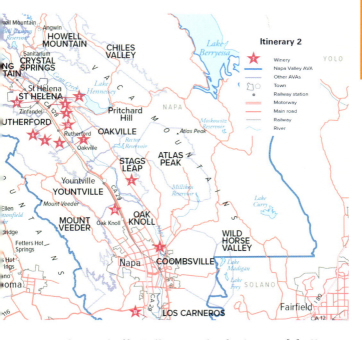

For history buffs, **Sullivan Rutherford Estate** [4] offers an architectural and cultural deep dive, while **Francis Ford Coppola's Inglenook** [5] is one of Napa Valley's most historic estates.

Bella Union [6] is a vibrant new addition to Napa Valley's Rutherford Bench. Part of **Far Niente's** family of wineries, it focuses primarily on Cabernet Sauvignon blends in a laid-back new tasting room.

Over in Oakville, drop into **Turnbull's** [7] fine old barn for single-vineyard Bordeaux wines sourced from their estate vineyards.

Wheeler Farms [8], off Zinfandel Lane in St Helena, owned by Suzanne Deal Booth, is a fully functioning farm with organic gardens, orchards and beehives, all integrated into its food and wine pairing experiences. Winemaker-

The Valley looking south, Chateau Montelena in the foreground

partner Nigel Kinsman's wines pair with the estate's farm-to-table offerings. Six minutes south, back in Rutherford, **Bella Oaks** [9], another of Booth's projects, reflects her deep ties to the arts. The property is both a vineyard and a gallery, with large-scale installations.

At **Louis M. Martini Winery** [10] in **St Helena**, book an experience that includes a food pairing or an underground tasting in the Martini wine cave. You'll find it enhances the wines in unexpected ways.

Step back in time at **Frank Family Vineyards** [11] off Larkmead Lane in **Calistoga**. Housed in a historic 1884 stone winery, it was once home to Larkmead Winery before being transformed by former Disney executive Rich Frank and his wife, Leslie. Today, it's a welcoming retreat where you can sip sparkling wines crafted by longtime winemaker Todd Graff – who once made bubbles at Schramsberg – alongside a diverse lineup of Chardonnays, Pinot Noirs and robust Cabernets. The porch is the perfect place to linger.

Where to Eat

Farmstead [12] at Long Meadow Ranch is the quintessential farm-to-table experience. The ranch itself supplies the organic produce, grass-fed beef and heirloom vegetables, resulting in a menu that feels hyper-seasonal and genuinely connected to Napa Valley's agricultural roots.

For dinner, try Thomas Keller's **Ad Hoc** in **Yountville** – the best night is Monday for their legendary fried chicken – or **Bear at Stanly Ranch** [13], where the cuisine is modern Californian: open-fire cooking, locally sourced ingredients and a seasonal menu.

Where to Stay

Calistoga Where you base yourself is important. **Four Seasons Napa Valley Resort & Residences** [14] in Calistoga is a blend of wine country luxury and laid-back elegance, with its own on-site winery, **Elusa**, making Bordeaux-inspired blends under the guidance of Thomas Rivers Brown and Jonathan Walden.

Yountville For something a little more groovy and intimate, **The Setting Inn** [15] — a hip, design-forward retreat between Oak Knoll and Yountville — offers bike rentals for cruising the nearby **Vine Trail**.

ITINERARY 3

Icons and legends

Throw a stone in Calistoga and St Helena and you'll hit an icon winery. In Calistoga, a visit to the ivy-covered **Chateau Montelena** [1] is essential for any Napa Valley pilgrim. Famous for its starring role in the Judgement of Paris (see p23) this fine estate, nestled in a quiet corner of Calistoga, still produces some of California's most elegant Cabernets and Chardonnays.

Nearby is the renowned sparkling wine house, **Schramsberg Vineyards** [2], a place steeped in history, from its hand-dug 19th-century caves to its famous 1972 Blanc de Blancs, served at Nixon's 1973 'Toast to Peace' with China. A visit here means immersing yourself in méthode traditionnelle winemaking.

On the Vine Trail

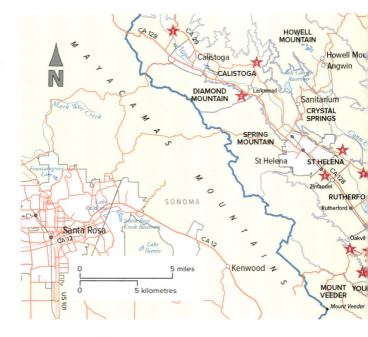

Hourglass [3] is a low-key but cult-status winery. Founder Jeff Smith and winemaker Tony Biagi make a portfolio of bold, expressive wines, all set to a rock-and-roll backdrop (on vinyl, of course).

Heading south to St Helena, you might book the Taste of Place experience at **Joseph Phelps Vineyards** [4], a 2.5-hour 'food and wine journey' including **Insignia**, one of Napa Valley's original Bordeaux blends.

Cathy Corison has been making elegant Cabernets for decades. Her **Corison Winery** [5], housed in an unassuming green-roofed barn off Highway 29 south of St Helena, is a haven of calm.

From Corison, you might zip down Zinfandel Lane, turn right onto Silverado Trail and head south toward a remarkable place – few wineries blend architecture, vineyard

and nature as seamlessly as **Quintessa** [6]. The biodynamically farmed estate in Rutherford, with its rolling, vine-covered hills, lake, and striking modern winery, runs outdoor tastings with panoramic views. The wines are among Napa Valley's most sought-after single-estate Bordeaux blends. The small-production **Illumination** Sauvignon Blanc is not to be missed.

Continuing south to **Oakville**, you'll see numerous gated driveways on the eastern or western flanks of the AVA. These lead to fabled estates: **Harlan Estate [7]**, **Bond**, **Promontory [8]**, **FUTO [9]**, **Screaming Eagle**, **Rudd**, **Opus One [10]**, **Cardinale [11]** and **Dalla Valle Vineyards**. See p112 for which of these you can visit.

Walk-ins are welcome at **PlumpJack Estate Winery [12]**. In the midst of the grand estates, this is one of Napa Valley's original cult wineries, a benchmark for opulent Cabernet Sauvignon. Founded by Gavin Newsom and Gordon Getty on an estate dating back to 1881, this Oakville gem continues to push the boundaries of richness and accessibility, producing wines that are hedonistic yet never overblown.

The Manor House, Stags' Leap Winery

South along Silverado Trail, keep a sharp eye out for **Pine Ridge Vineyards [13]**, in the steep, terraced hills of Stags Leap District. Blink, and you'll pass right by the Cabernet powerhouse producer, whose wines balance power with finely etched minerality. The Chenin Blanc Viognier blend is a crisp, floral contrast to their structured reds.

If one wine defines Napa Valley's rise to global prestige, it's **Shafer Vineyards**' **[14]** Hillside Select, a 100% Cabernet Sauvignon sourced from the winery's Stags Leap District estate. First released in 1983, Hillside Select set a new standard for single-vineyard Cabernet Sauvignon, proving that Napa Valley's best sites could produce wines that rivalled the world's finest Grand Crus. Nearby **Stags' Leap Winery [15]** — founded in 1893 — is one of the valley's most historically significant (and slightly spooky) estates, known for lush, intensely structured reds; it's renowned for its Petite Sirah.

Returning to the Silverado Trail and south you'll find **Stag's Leap Wine Cellars [16]** and **Clos du Val [17]** in the Stags Leap District AVA — sacred ground for icon status Cabernet lovers and veterans of the Paris Tasting (see p23). They remain benchmarks for classically styled Napa Cabernet.

Where to Eat

Calistoga Take a dip in the pool or hot tub before a Michelin-starred, hyper-seasonal dinner at **Auro.**

Try to score a seat by the fireplace at **Sam's Social Club**, a lively New American restaurant at **Indian Springs Resort**, or wrap up around the fire pit at **Robert's Tropical Table**. **St Helena** For something more laid-back, head to **Gott's Roadside** (the original location is in St Helena, and there's one in Napa near the **Oxbow Market**) for a Vietnamese chicken salad, a Kale Caesar, or a superb burger – and don't miss the locally made Straus Family Creamery ice cream.

For sunset drinks, then dinner, **Auberge du Soleil** remains one of the most magical dining destinations in the valley. Perched high above **Rutherford Hill**, its breathtaking views and French-Californian cuisine make it a place to savour slowly.

The historic **Oakville Grocery**, owned by Jean-Charles Boisset of **Raymond Vineyards** and **Buena Vista Winery** fame, has been a wine country institution since 1881. Grab a wood-fired pizza and a seat outside, and browse the wine list. The **Oakville Wine Merchant** next door has 85 wines by the glass, and many more to buy.

Where to Stay

Calistoga Check into the ultra-luxe **Solage**.
Rutherford The intimate, vineyard-ringed **Rancho Caymus Inn** is in a beautifully restored hacienda.
Stags Leap District For spectacular sunset views, the **Poetry Inn**, perched high above Stags Leap Palisades, offers some of the most exclusive accommodations in Napa.

Gott's Roadside, St Helena

ITINERARY 4
Downtown Napa on foot

Start the day with an early morning hot air balloon ride over the valley with **Napa Valley Aloft Hot Air Balloon Rides** (book at nvaloft.com), then set out on foot to explore the bustling heart of Napa city, where tasting rooms, wine bars, restaurants and upscale shops line the streets.

Or another great way to start your day is at the lively **Oxbow Public Market**. Grab an espresso and pastry from **Ritual Coffee**, a fresh-pressed juice from **Hudson Greens & Goods** or a Pastrami, Egg and Cheese from **Loveski**, the bagel shop by Michelin-starred chef Christopher Kostow and his wife, Martina.

The Downtown Tasting Trail

For more detail see Best Downtown Napa tasting rooms p192

From Oxbow, take a leisurely walk through downtown Napa, where tasting rooms are plentiful, each offering a different take on Napa Valley's winemaking scene.

Benevolent Neglect – Known for small-batch, experimental winemaking.

Mayacamas Downtown – A downtown extension of one of Napa's historic mountain wineries (see p93).

The River Club – An intimate tasting experience with limited-production wines.

Wine retailers (see Napa Valley wine shops

Outer Space Wines

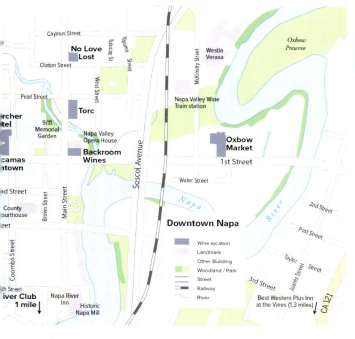

p158) include **Backroom Wines**, a wine shop featuring international selections and Napa Valley rarities, and **Maison Fayard**, which has a rotating selection of wines by winemaker Julien Fayard. **Outer Space Wines**, with its astro-themed décor, serves daily flights of local wines alongside cheese plates and wine-friendly snacks.

The number of walk-in tasting rooms in Napa has exploded, giving visitors many choices: **JaM Cellars**, **Krupp Brothers**, **Vermeil Wines**, **WALT Wines**, **John Anthony Vineyards**, **Vineyard 29**, **Chateau Buena Vista**, **Alpha Omega Collective**, **Ackerman Family Vineyards** at **The Heritage House**, **Keplinger Wines** and many more.

For a laid-back, end-of-day tasting, visit **No Love Lost**, where winemaker Jay Nunez serves up lean Chardonnays,

Zinfandels and Rieslings, or pop into **Cadet Wine & Beer**, which has a menu of bites to accompany their selection of rare Champagnes, California wines and... beer.

Where to Eat

Lunch: **The Fatted Calf** at Oxbow for sandwich specials, savoury tarts and home-prepared charcuterie. **Model Bakery** has huge slices of sourdough pizza, made with a starter cultivated from wine grape fermentations; **Loveski** for Matzoh Ball Soup or Chicken Schnitzel; rich chowder at **Hog Island Oyster Co. Croccante** is a must for Neapolitan-style pizza; **Stateline Road Smokehouse**, for an authentic, no-frills barbecue. **Scala Osteria & Bar** brings an Amalfi Coast energy to downtown Napa, serving elevated southern Italian seafood and handmade pastas.

For dinner, **Torc** is a favourite among Napa Valley winemakers. Think freshly-shaved truffle over homemade pasta, grilled meats and peak-season produce. The 20-page wine list includes deep verticals of Napa Valley icons.

Where to stay

Prefer downtown charm? **The Archer Hotel** and nearby **Andaz Napa** place you right in the heart of the action, while just outside town going south, the **Stanly Ranch, Auberge Resorts Collection** is spacious and luxurious.

Things to do in Napa Valley besides wine

Napa Valley might be one of the world's greatest wine regions, but it's also a place of spectacular natural beauty, with a fascinating history. From fishing, hiking and swimming in the lovely Bothe-Napa State Park, to learning more about Napa Valley's Native American culture in Yountville's excellent little museum, to sculpture gardens and gastronomic marvels, there's a wealth of things to do beyond the ever-interesting and all-consuming subject of wine...

Sterling Vineyards Gondola, Calistoga

Calistoga

Sterling Vineyards

1111 Dunaweal Lane, Calistoga

Besides its excellent Bordeaux varietal wines, Sterling has an aerial gondola that takes visitors on a thrilling ride 300 feet above the valley floor. There are other tastings and tours available, but the $95 Hilltop Experience – a ride on the gondola and a tasting – is highly recommended.

sterlingvineyards.com

Castello di Amorosa

4045 St Helena Highway

Dario Sattui spent a fortune importing antiques to fill his 14th century-style, Tuscan-inspired castle complete with battlements, towers, 107 rooms and a dungeon where they serve Italian-inspired wines (and grape juice for the kids).

castellodiamorosa.com

Calistoga Depot

1458 Lincoln Avenue

This historic train depot is a tribute to Calistoga founder and businessman Sam Brannan. Guests can taste wine or spirits from the distillery on site, dine on tacos or caviar or pick up gifts in the shop. calistogadepot.com

Old Faithful Geyser of California

1299 Tubbs Lane

It's not as dramatic as Yellowstone's Old Faithful but Calistoga's geyser, which erupts every 15 to 30 minutes, is spectacular nevertheless. The $15 fee includes entry to the park and petting zoo.

calistogaspa.com/things-to-do/old-faithful-geyser

St Helena
Bale Grist Mill State Historic Park

3369 St. Helena Highway

An 1846 water-powered mill that ground grain into flour was a community hub for early settlers in the valley – the park also contains Napa Valley's first church and Pioneer Cemetery. It's open at weekends for milling demonstrations, historical tours and hiking. You can take the 2.4 mile History Trail that connects to Bothe-Napa Valley State Park. $8

napaoutdoors.org/parks/bale-grist-mill-state-historic-park

Bothe-Napa Valley State Park

3801 St Helena Highway North, Calistoga

This state park, open daily from 8am to sunset, has hiking trails, fishing, a pool, redwood forests and creeks, and cabins and yurts for overnight stays. The Calistoga-St Helena vine trail runs through here. Hike or bike in free, with a small charge for cars.

napaoutdoors.org/parks/bothe-napa-valley-state-park

Bunny Foo-Foo at Hall Wines

401 St Helena Highway South

The 11-metre stainless steel hare leaping into the sky is a sculpture that makes Hall, with its diverse selection of well-made wines, hard to miss. The property blends historic and modern buildings punctuated with striking art. Tastings start at $40 and tours at $60.

hallwines.com/hall-schedule-a-tour-and-tasting

Culinary Institute of America at Greystone

2555 Main Street

The West coast headquarters of the CIA (Culinary Institute of America) offers hands-on cooking classes and demonstrations, dining in two restaurants, a small culinary museum and gift shop in the magnificent stone mansion that was once the Christian Brothers Winery.

ciachef.edu/cia-california-admissions-tours-and-events

Oakville
Oakville Grocery

7856 St. Helena Highway

A lovely piece of old Napa Valley, the 1881 gourmet grocery has been a popular stop for hungry travellers for nearly 150 years. Pop in for prepared foods, sandwiches made to order or a bottle of wine. Upstairs there is a museum of Napa Valley Wine History.

oakvillegrocery.com

Welcome to Napa Valley Sign

7602 St Helena Highway

First erected in 1949 (and little changed since then) this vintage carved redwood sign with vineyards and mountains in the background is a popular picture spot, especially during winter mustard season. It's on Highway 29 between Yountville and Oakville. There is an identical sign at the northern end of the valley near Calistoga, just across from Cardinale.

Yountville
Napa Valley Museum Yountville

55 Presidents' Circle

This little museum tucked away in Yountville hosts a range of exhibits including art by valley residents. Permanent galleries are dedicated to the geological make-up of the valley, and its history from the original Native American inhabitants. Adult admission is $20 for non-members.

napavalleymuseum.org/visit

Napa city
Culinary Institute of America at Copia

500 1st Street

Dine in the student-run cafe, try a cookery or wine class, peruse the David and Judy Breitstein Collection of historic wines or pick up gifts. Don't miss the two-storey abstract mural of 'food as art.'

ciaatcopia.com

The Oxbow Public Market

610 + 644 1st Street

This food hall is packed with every kind of eatery for every taste and every pocket, from the Fatted Calf charcuterie, Model Bakery and Gott's Roadside, to tacos and wood-fired pizza, pastrami sandwiches and freshly caught oysters and sweets including cookies, cupcakes and artisan ice cream. Find a seat inside or out.

oxbowpublicmarket.com

Mt Veeder
Hess Persson Estates Winery and Art Museum

4411 Redwood Road, Napa, CA 94558

This Mt Veeder winery has a gallery with an impressive

contemporary art collection including pieces by Robert Rauschenberg, Andy Goldsworthy and Francis Bacon, curated over three decades by winery founder Donald Hess. Tastings and tours, some with three course menus, start at $125.

hesspersonestates.com

Los Carneros
di Rosa Center for Contemporary Art

5200 Sonoma Highway, Napa

Explore two galleries full of contemporary art set in a natural setting that includes walking trails, a lake and picnic grounds. $25 for a ticket.
dirosaart.org

Donum

24500 Ramal Road, Sonoma

On the Sonoma side of Carneros, Donum winery is one of the world's most extensive sculpture gardens, the vines punctuated by more than 60 giant works from the world's great artists. Installations include Ai Weiwei's Circle of Animals/Zodiac Heads and Crouching Spider by Louise Bourgeois, among many site-specific commissions. Stunning.

thedonumestate.com

A sensory dream trip through Napa Valley

Spend a fabulous weekend in wine country with Jean-Charles Boisset, who has curated a collection of properties that embellish your journey with theatricality, history, and sensory indulgence.

Our commitment to excellence extends beyond the glass (and table), with our knowledgeable and charismatic teams helping you create lasting memories to be shared with friends and family.

Unparalleled experiences await you across Napa Valley. From Calistoga to Napa, Boisset Collection offers a treasure trove of delights for our guests in every corner of the Valley.

Our vision is to enlighten, inspire, surprise and transport you to destinations you've never imagined. Experience Napa Valley through the mind and inspiration of **Jean-Charles' Perfect Day**.

- Experience distilling, brewing and winemaking the 1868 way at the **Calistoga Depot**
- Discover the wines of Jean-Charles' home of Burgundy, alongside the lush wines of Napa Valley at **JCB St Helena**

Jean-Charles Boisset

JCB St Helena

Calistoga Depot

Chateau Buena Vista, Napa

- Make your own wine at the historic **Raymond Vineyards**
- Celebrate history with over 80 wines by the glass at the **Oakville Wine Merchant**, part of the iconic 1881 **Oakville Grocery**
- Visit **Elizabeth Spencer Winery** at the 1872 post office in Rutherford
- Unite Napa Valley wines, luxury and style at **JCB Yountville**
- Finish your day at **Chateau Buena Vista** tasting room in downtown Napa with the ultimate indulgence: Champagne, caviar, Cabernet and chocolate

Follow this link for your journey with Jean-Charles in Napa Valley
jcbcollection.com/visit-us/wine-country

Content supported by Boisset Collection

How to visit an elite winery

They may be legends of the wine world, but many of Napa Valley's most famous wineries aren't open to the public. Visiting them calls for prep work – plus, of course, a little insider knowledge.

Realm Cellars

As you plan your Napa Valley trip, you may wonder if there's a way to visit Screaming Eagle, Harlan, or other legendary Napa Valley names. Sadly, the answer to that question is no. Unless you know someone at the winery or you've been on the allocation list for years, most of what used to be called 'cult' wineries are closed to visitors. Screaming Eagle doesn't even have a sign at the almost-hidden turn off the Silverado Trail.

Many of Napa Valleys's exclusive wineries are tiny and lack the tasting space or staff to welcome visitors. Others are purely winemaking operations without the permits needed to welcome guests. And nobody wants to flout regulations: in 2024 Napa County fined a small winery $8m for allegedly violating the rules.There are those vintners who have perfected that balance between exclusivity and hospitality. Here's how to start the conversation.

Calistoga
Realm Cellars

Realm North, 1171 Tubbs Lane, Calistoga, CA 94515

Scott Becker's first career was in military intelligence. He came to Napa Valley in the mid-2000s, worked under Jack Cakebread and Bill Harlan, and acquired Realm with then partner Benoit Touquette in 2012. Their vision was to develop a collection of high-end blends and single-site wines, each from a notable terroir. Realm owns a handful of properties including the Moonracer estate in Stags Leap District and Houyi on Pritchard Hill. Visitors are invited to the Realm North tasting room in Calistoga, a beautiful indoor/outdoor lounge and art gallery hung with label artwork, and with amazing views of the Vaca Mountains. From Fidelio Sauvignon Blanc, to Air Earth Water from Pritchard Hill, the wines are considered examples of the finest modern Napa Valley: marvels of precision, intensity and balance. Guests need an appointment which can be booked on the website or by contacting the team via email or phone. For other bookable events, see the Experience section of their website.

realmcellars.com/experience

St Helena
Accendo Cellars

Wheeler Farms

588 Zinfandel Lane, St Helena, CA 94574

After cult wine pioneers Bart and Daphne Araujo sold their famed Eisele Vineyard in 2013 to the group that owns Chateau Latour, they created a new family wine brand called Accendo with their children Jaime and Greg. During an immersive 90-minute experience at the Wheeler Farms Winery property in St Helena, guests tour the apiary, chicken coops, fruit and flower gardens and vineyard. The visit culminates in a seated tasting of five wines made by winemakers Françoise Peschon and Nigel Kinsman, with artisan cheeses and surprises from the garden. The $160-per person tasting fee is waived with an appropriate purchase.

accendocellars.com

Melka Estates

2900 Silverado Trail N, St Helena, CA 94574

You will almost certainly have drunk a Melka wine and not known it. Philippe Melka and his wife Cherie, and their team of seven full-time winemakers, produce about 100,000 cases for some 34 clients from Santa Barbara to Washington State, Chile, Australia and Mexico. The Napa Valley client list includes Alejandro Bulgheroni Estate, Davis Estates, Raymond Vineyards, Tusk, Westwood; over the years Melka has worked with Dalla Valle, Bryant, Quintessa and Hundred Acre. Their headquarters is a functional and rather beautiful steel-walled winery in St Helena,

Melka Estates

where they combine 'home, lifestyle and business,' as Melka says. If you want to visit, email Sylvie Laly, vice-president of sales, to make an appointment. The tasting includes five wines from the Melka portfolio, for $165 per person. A three-bottle purchase waives the fee.

melkaestates.com

Oakville
MacDonald Vineyards

P.O. Box 91, Oakville, CA 94562

Graeme MacDonald (pictured, left) and his brother Alex are growers first, but the former has established his talents in the cellar, making wines for Gandona and Blankiet. For his family label based on estate fruit from the historic To Kalon vineyard, Graeme MacDonald strips away the artifice and extras like lots of new French oak, so the fruit and the prime vineyard come to the fore. They don't receive guests at their vineyard, but Alex can arrange tastings. Email info@macdonaldvineyards.com or call 707-225-7264 to inquire.

macdonaldvineyards.com

Promontory

1601 Oakville Grade, Oakville, CA 94562

The sister winery to Harlan estate, Promontory is an extraordinary, untamed mountain property in a deep valley folded into the foothills of Mount Veeder. Bill Harlan first discovered it in the 1980s while hiking along Oakville's southwestern ridge. Tastings are at the striking Howard Backen-designed winery hidden behind

a mighty oxidized iron gate off Oakville Cross Road. The 90-minute session is $300 per person and includes a glass of Dom Perignon on arrival, a tour with a barrel tasting of a young vintage in the cellar, and a seated tasting of two vintages. By appointment only; the winery recommends reserving well in advance, as there is a wait list especially in the peak months.

www.promontorywine.com

Futo Estate

1575 Oakville Grade Rd, Oakville, CA 94562

Futo is a hidden gem, a splendid modern winery (from the atelier of Howard Backen, Napa Valley's most celebrated architect), surrounded by terraced vineyards. The team that runs this boutique winery is tiny: they don't have a hospitality person, and winemaker Jason Exposto is also the vineyard manager, ensuring absolute precision from grape to glass. Most visit requests are fielded from those on the mailing list, though interested parties can call (+1) 707-944-9333 to enquire. 'We try to see wine lovers when we can,' Exposto says. It's well worth the effort – the views are superb and the wines, from Oakville and Stags Leap District, are considered among the finest expressions of modern Napa Valley.

futoestate.com

Opus One

7900 St Helena Highway, Oakville, CA 94562

With its futuristic cupola, grass-covered sides and white walls, Opus One resembles a citadel on a hill. One of the landmarks on Highway 29, a monument to the 1978 Franco-American partnership of Baron Philippe de Rothschild and Robert Mondavi, this fine building (it's as compelling inside

Opus One

as out) is about to celebrate its half-century. The Opus One Experience, in a richly appointed space with panoramic vineyard views, starts with tea in delicate hand-fired pottery before a series of wines including the current vintage and a library wine, paired with exquisite bites. The 90-minute visit is $200, new appointment slots are released on the first of the month, and reservations are available up to two months in advance.

opusonewinery.com

Detert Family Vineyards

Tasting room at Dakota Shy Wine, 771 Sage Canyon Road, St Helena, CA 94574

Winemaker Tom Garrett and his brother inherited an old farmhouse and a Cabernet Franc vineyard in To Kalon (their cousins, the McDonalds, got the part planted to Cabernet Sauvignon). Though they can't use that famous name (the rights to To Kalon have been mired in legal wranglings for years), they make some of the most sought-after Cabernet Franc in the valley. Tastings of three to seven wines (costing $125 to $175) take place at Dakota Shy (Garrett's other brand) in a chic, rustic room with a view of barrels and sky. To arrange a tasting, complete the form on the Dakota Shy website or email info@detert.com.

detert.com

Tasting barn, Brion

Yountville
Brion

PO Box 471 Napa, California 94559

Brion (pronounced as 'Brian') Wise is a restless entrepreneur who started his own energy company at the age of 26, grew cotton in Australia, developed a titanium bicycle chain, opened a restaurant and wine bar, bought land in Sonoma's Moon Mountain District and now makes wines from Oregon to Russian River to Champagne. Under his BRION label he makes single vineyard Napa Valley Cabernet Sauvignons from his Pritchard Hill estate vineyard in St Helena, Sleeping Lady Vineyard in Yountville and Caldwell Vineyard in Coombsville. You can visit his 1870s-era gravity winery and tasting lounge in Yountville, a showpiece salon filled with fine art. The visit starts with a flute of Brion Wise Côte de Blancs Champagne and includes a look at the Sleeping Lady Vineyard. The tasting lounge is by reservation only, although most guests come through referrals. The fee is $150 per person; a three-bottle purchase waives the fee.

brionwines.com bwisevineyards.com/visit

Mount Veeder
Pott Wine

2272 Mt Veeder Road, Napa, CA 94558

Aaron Pott is a master of the Bordeaux varietals with an

Pott Wine

impeccable CV. After degrees from UC Davis and the Université de Bourgogne in Dijon, he worked for John Kongsgaard at Newton on Spring Mountain, then went back to France in 1993, where he was winemaker at Château Troplong-Mondot in St Emilion, then director of winemaking at La Tour Figeac. In 1998 he returned to Napa Valley to head up Quintessa in Rutherford. Now he makes single vineyard wines (from famous vineyards like Stagecoach and Lagier-Meredith) and Cabernet Sauvignon blends, with evocative names like Incubo, Dynamite with a Laser Beam, Her Majesty's Secret Service and Original Gangster. To visit, sign up first for his allocation list email, and then write to his business partner and wife Claire with your request. Guests tour the Pott Wines Mount Veeder property, then sit down in the Potts' artsy ranch home with a view for a tasting of his entire range. The tasting is complimentary.

pottwine.com

Pritchard Hill
OVID

255 Long Ranch Rd, St Helena, CA 94574

The wonders of the natural world and the beauty of Pritchard Hill are central to the experience at Ovid. Winemaker Austin Peterson works his stony vineyards 430m above Oakville (they took out 50,000 cubic metres of rock when they planted in 1998) to create wines of astonishing precision and freshness. The tasting room is magnificent, a symphony

Tasting room, Ovid

of wood and stone with a vast picture window over the vineyards. The tasting and tour cost $300; purchasing six bottles of Experiment or three bottles of Hexameter or OVID waives the fee. To arrange a tasting, email reservations@ovidnapavalley.com. Virtual tastings can also be arranged.

ovidnapavalley.com

Coombsville
Covert Estate

15 Chateau Lane, Napa, CA 94558

As the name implies, Covert Estate is a bit under the radar. Winemaker Julien Fayard, who worked at two Bordeaux châteaux, Lafite Rothschild and Smith Haut Lafitte, before an eight-year stint with Philippe Melka (see p114), is well-known for his wine consulting projects including Somnium, Le Pich, Nicholson Jones and Purlieu. Covert Estate, a winery which 'sits underground between the vineyard and the oak grove, and can only be seen from a bird's-eye view', is his personal think tank and modernist winemaking space, and it offers a glimpse into his personality, and his devotion to the most sophisticated equipment. The experience includes a cave tour and tasting of three Covert Estate Cabernet Sauvignon wines in a striking indoor-outdoor

Favia Wines, Coombsville

salon designed by Richard von Saal. A three-bottle purchase waives one $150 per person tasting fee.

covertestate.com

The Salon, Covert Estate

Favia Wines

2031 Coombsville Road, Napa CA 94558

Winemaker Andy Erickson and his viticulturist wife Annie Favia have worked with some of the best names in Napa Valley: Harlan Estate, Screaming Eagle, Mayacamas, Corison, Kongsgaard and David Abreu among many others. For all that, their unassuming house and delightful garden feel a hundred miles from the glamorous hustle of St Helena and its neighbours. Their tastings offer a glimpse into down-to-earth Coombsville: the $90 private experience starts with Línea Sauvignon Blanc and a tour of the gardens (a cornucopia of fruit, vegetables and herbs, many of which are for Annie's organic tea company ERDA). The tasting in the 1886 stone cellar explores Coombsville and Oakville AVAs through a pair of Cabernet Sauvignons plus Cabernet Franc-dominant blends.

faviawines.com

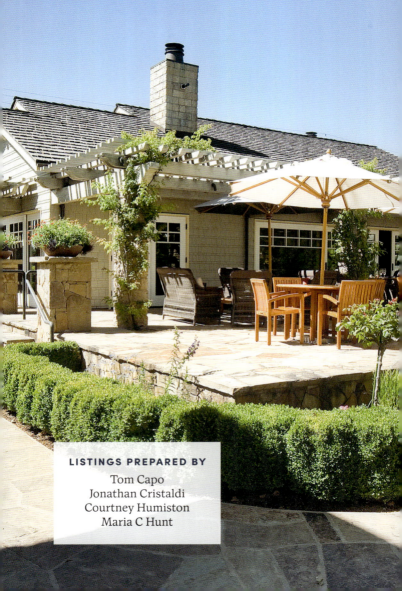

Cliff Lede Vineyards, Yountville

LISTINGS PREPARED BY

Tom Capo
Jonathan Cristaldi
Courtney Humiston
Maria C Hunt

The Guide

Contents

Napa Valley winery tours and tastings	124
Napa Valley hotels for wine lovers	136
Fine dining in Napa Valley	148
Napa Valley wine shops	158
Napa Valley wineries with great food	170
Napa Valley wine bars	182
Downtown Napa tasting rooms	192

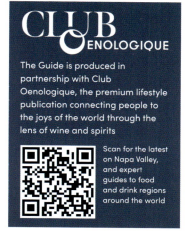

CLUB OENOLOGIQUE

The Guide is produced in partnership with Club Oenologique, the premium lifestyle publication connecting people to the joys of the world through the lens of wine and spirits

Scan for the latest on Napa Valley, and expert guides to food and drink regions around the world

Napa Valley winery tours and tastings

Wine lovers have been flocking to Napa Valley's wineries for nearly 150 years – so they've had some time to work out what people want from a tasting room. Here we list 20 wineries up and down the valley that welcome visitors. Almost all require reservations.

Tasting room, Adamvs

Despite wine having a history dating back to 6,000 BCE, the pastime of wine tasting is a very recent novelty. For much of its California-based history, wine has been an agricultural byproduct sold by the jug by farmers, along with eggs, prunes and walnuts. That all changed thanks to Charles Krug, a Prussian immigrant and winemaker who opened California's very first tasting room in 1882. The idea caught on and more Napa Valley wineries followed suit, introducing tasting opportunities to offer their visitors. Allowing people to sample wines, compare the flavours and decide which ones they like the best has helped to elevate the drink to an artisanal level and today, wine tasting in Napa Valley is big business, bringing 3.7 million visitors to the valley in 2023.

'Perch on a pretty patio, get cosy in a wine cave, see the scenery from the back of a motorized cart or settle into an architecturally significant salon'

You'll find every kind of wine tasting to fit your mood, palate and personality. Perch on a pretty patio, get cosy in a wine cave, see the scenery from the back of a motorized cart or settle into an architecturally significant salon for wines paired with haute cuisine. Expect to pay tasting fees of $50 to $80, with many high-end wineries charging upwards of $125 per person depending on the experience. A few places accommodate walk-in guests, but most wineries require reservations, especially on weekends.

If you're short on time, the tasting rooms of downtown Napa (see p192) focus on sipping wine in a beautiful – and more conveniently located – space.

But if you're keen to learn more about some of the world's most enticing wine labels from grape to glass, here's a selection of leading Napa Valley wineries where you should prioritize a visit.

Where winemakers dine

For luxury-tier fine dining, I'm going with **Kenzo**. Think about precision cuisine like The French Laundry but with Japanese style. It is unbelievable. For multi-course, luxury dining, it's probably my favourite place in the United States right now. It is truly a gastronomic journey, and one that changes all the time. The last time I dined, there was of course some sashimi – but then they went into some beautiful root vegetable dishes and we had some wagyu. We had the wine pairings, which included wine and sake, which was so much fun – and I love Champagne, so we ordered that, too.

It's very refined and intimate. If you go with an engaged group keen for wonderful dialogue and with exploratory desires when it comes to cuisine, you're going to have an unbelievable night.

Rob Mondavi Jr, Rutledge and Vine

Calistoga

LOLA
916 Foothill Blvd. Calistoga CA 94515

Seth Cripe of LOLA is in the vanguard of a new generation of winemakers creating flawless, acid-driven wines using classic plus underappreciated grape varieties from heritage vineyards. Tastings at Lola's cosy cottage, complete with wood-burning fireplace, may include Chenin Blanc, Albariño, Charbono, Zinfandel and Pinot Noir made using minimal-intervention techniques. Consider adding some of the house-made bottarga (cured fish roe) to your tasting experience.

lolawines.com

Schramsberg Vineyards
1400 Schramsberg Road, Calistoga CA 94515

Winemaker Jessica Koga and CEO Hugh Davies carry on the Schramsberg tradition of making fine American méthode champenoise wines with Chardonnay and Pinot Noir. Hugh's parents, Jack and Jamie Davies, pioneered that style in California in 1965. From the blanc de blancs to the brut rosé, it's easy to see why these balanced, creamy and vibrant wines have been enjoyed repeatedly by world leaders and politicians at the White House in Washington DC. Seeing the circa-1862 Victorian house and touring the slightly spooky hand-dug caves are a must when visiting Napa Valley.

schramsberg.com

Howell Mountain

Adamvs

501 White Cottage road North Angwin, CA

A team of winery cows and herbal preparations help viticulturist Mike Wolf nurture the land at Denise

and Stephen Adams' modern biodynamic wine estate, Adamvs (pronounced uh-DAM-us), named in Latin as a reference to the red clay earth. Consultant Philippe Melka and winemaker Alberto Bianchi's ethereal wines, including Quintus, Téres and Adamus, capture the essence of the estate's soils. Touring the site in a vintage Land Rover with electric engine and tasting in the modern glass-walled space surrounded by a freestanding cypress log sculpture, guests are invited to commune with nature as well as with these unique wines.

adamvs.com

St Helena

La Sirena Winery

4455 St Helena Hwy, Calistoga, CA 94515

Heidi Peterson Barrett is the queen of Napa Valley's 100-point winemaking consultants. At her La Sirena tasting room, Barrett offers her signature balanced and intensely flavoured Cabs (including those from the Barrett & Barrett label, a collaboration with her husband Bo Barrett), as well as wines from other grape varieties she loves, including Syrah, Amador County Primitivo and Calistoga Muscat. Visiting the rustic vineyard house, decorated with Barrett's original oil paintings, offers a chance to acquire wines from all her brands.

lasirenawine.com

Stony Hill Vineyard
3331 St Helena Hwy North, St Helena, CA 94574

Founders Fred and Eleanor McCrea used to entertain guests at their Spring Mountain home to showcase their singular white wines. Under the ownership of Lawrence Wine Estates since 2021, Stony Hill has since instituted biodynamic viticulture and carried out a renovation that honours the 1951 home's mid-century origins, creating unique residential tasting spaces. Guests on the elevated Terroir Experience explore the land in a Lexus GX 550 before tasting winemaker Reid Griggs' mineral-driven Chardonnay and Cabernet Sauvignon matured by the magnum.

stonyhillvineyard.com

Corison Winery
987 St. Helena Hwy, St Helena CA 94574

Cathy Corison is a pioneering winemaker and purist, making Cabernet Sauvignon in restrained style inspired by Bordeaux. Her flagship Cab Sauvs plus Cabernet Franc wines come from Sunbasket and Kronos estate vineyards, and she also makes rosé, Gewurztraminer and Riesling under her Corazón label. The

Stony Hill

Corison Winery

unfussy, by-appointment tasting experience carried out in the working wine cellar or on the patio is as pure and elemental as the wines. Corison's daughter Grace now assists with winemaking ensuring that the family winery will endure.

corison.com

Spottswoode Winery
1902 Madrona Ave. St Helena CA 94574

The heart of Spottswoode is the organic- and biodynamic-certified vineyard that teems with birds, wildflowers and so much life. Founder Mary Novak and her daughters have made it a benchmark for pure wines with a sense of place, from expressive Sauvignon Blanc to lushly balanced Cabernet Sauvignon. Email or call to reserve a private tasting experience at the historic estate dating back to 1882. For the Then and Now tasting, the host greets guests with a glass of Mary's Block Sauvignon Blanc before a guided tour of the vineyard, sampling from the barrel and a seated tasting of library wine.

spottswoode.com

Tres Sabores
1620 S. Whitehall Lane, St Helena, CA 94574

Guests see the constant buzz of activity at Tres Sabores, from bottling to planting cover crops to welcoming a baby lamb. Julie Johnson and husband John Engelskirger run a certified-organic farm with sheep, goats, gardens and pomegranate trees. Grab a seat in the garden and enjoy wines that are bright and full of personality, from a Rhône white blend and Zinfandel rosé to bright and juicy Cabernet Franc and Petite Sirah. The new Insight Tour and Tasting Experience offers a deeper exploration into organic grape growing,

Spottswoode Winery

biodiversity and how animals nurture the vineyard, plus a comparative tasting of wine from the barrel and the library.

tressabores.com

Cathiard Vineyard
1978 Zinfandel Lane, St Helena, CA 94574

Bordelaise sensibility and California terroir meet at Cathiard Vineyard, a winery by Florence and Daniel Cathiard, the family behind Smith Haut-Lafitte in Pessac-Léognan. By-appointment tastings start with a splash of white Bordeaux from the mothership, before a jaunt around the property and vineyards in a restored Land Rover with an electric engine. Enjoy a trio of wines – Hora, Cathiard and Founding Brothers – from their estate vineyards at the foot of the Mayacamas Mountains. Tastings are hosted on a terrace with a view across the valley, as weather permits, or in a study filled with French antiques. It's the only winery in the valley with a dedicated cooperage and French-trained cooper working on-site.

cathiardvineyard.com

Rutherford

Inglenook
1991 St. Helena Hwy, Rutherford CA 94573

Founded in 1879, Inglenook is one of the historic properties

Inglenook

Rudd Estate

that helped put Napa Valley wine on the international map. Filmmaker Francis Ford Coppola of *Godfather* fame took over in 1975 and the family restored the property, even adding a film museum. More recently, Philippe Bascaules of Château Margaux was hired to direct the winemaking of gems like Rubicon and its Blancaneaux white blend. A plethora of tasting options offer cellar tours, seated tastings or the chance to enjoy wines with Mediterranean dishes from the bistro.

inglenook.com

Oakville

Rudd Estate

500 Oakville Cross Road, Oakville, CA 94562

Tucked away off the Silverado Trail, Rudd Estate is a singular wine ecosystem where an experience full of exquisite details awaits. Visitors tour the biodynamic vineyards, gardens and a workshop (aka winery) with Bordeaux-style concrete tanks before settling in for a private tasting in the greenhouse, at the harvest table or in a boathouse overlooking a small lake. Winemaker Natalie Bath uses native yeasts and a variety of tanks for her memorable and distinctive wines of place including an Oakville Estate red that's earthy with bright berries, and the Mt Veeder Estate Leslie's Blend brimming with dark, savoury umami and herbs.

ruddwines.com

Pritchard Hill

Chappellet Winery

1581 Sage Canyon Road, St Helena, CA 94574

Chappellet's oxidised iron pyramid seems like it just grew out of the ground among the ferns, moss and mature trees on Pritchard Hill. This is one of the Valley's most acclaimed spots for Cabernet Sauvignon, and the Chappellets have been learning the terroir since 1967. Depending on the experience, guests will taste from a barrel,

Chappellet

Domaine Chandon

explore older vintages or tour the property in a four-wheel drive vehicle. From Chenin Blanc to the Pritchard Hill icon wine, winemaker Philip Corallo-Titus crafts ageworthy wines that capture freshness and acidity.

chappellet.com

Yountville

Domaine Chandon

1 California Drive Yountville, CA 94599

Domaine Chandon was the first outpost from a Champagne maker in Napa Valley, and the circa-1970s winery fits seamlessly into the landscape. A 2023 renovation brought biophilic interior design and outdoor tasting spaces that showcase the Yountville setting. Book a sparkling lunch tasting starring fried chicken, or groups of 6-to-12 may reserve a private garden cabana to sip rosé from magnum as a parade of dishes appear. Some walk-ins are accepted, but reservations are wise.

chandon.com

Stags Leap District

Quixote Winery

6126 Silverado Trail, Napa CA 94558

Quixote Winery, as the name hints, is a fanciful estate inspired by the quest of Miguel de Cervantes' most famous character. Founder Carl Doumani wanted to create a playful winery with turrets, curves and tile mosaics to showcase serious Cabernet Sauvignon and Petite Sirah made from mountain fruit. Architecture buffs won't want to miss a chance to spend time in the only North American building by Austrian painter and architect Friedensreich Hundertwasser.

quixotewinery.com

Quixote Winery

Shafer Vineyards

Mt Brave

Shafer Vineyards
6154 Silverado Trail Napa, CA 94558

Shafer's Hillside Select is one of the Napa Valley icon wines that collectors covet. Winemaker Elias Fernandez is a master at creating wines with power, balance and from the hillside vineyards first planted by founder John Shafer in the 1970s. Of the three tasting experiences, the most luxe is the Hillside Select Experience, which includes Billecart-Salmon Champagne and Regiis Ova caviar, a vineyard tour in a Polaris Ranger, and finally, a seated tasting of 5-, 10- and 20-year-old library wines.

shafervineyards.com

Mount Veeder

Mt Brave
3875 Mt Veeder Road, Napa CA 94558

From a perch more than 1,400 feet above the valley floor, guests feel on top of the world at Mt Brave. The signature, by-appointment Mt Veeder Experience includes a greeting at the front of the estate, a visit to a scenic lookout and a seated tasting in a glam furnished tent with a view of the vineyard and mountains. Guests enjoy Mt Brave wines that may include Cabernet Sauvignon, Malbec and a Chenin Blanc blend, as well as others from 100-point winemaker Chris Carpenter's portfolio such as La Jota and Hickinbotham from South Australia's McLaren Vale.

mtbravewines.com

Oak Knoll

Robert Biale Vineyards
4038 Big Ranch Road, Napa CA 94558

Biale's many remarkable and refined Zinfandels are wonders that will win over anyone who's ever doubted the merits of the grape variety so closely tied to California. Fruit is grown in their estate vineyards as well as some of California's most acclaimed heritage vineyards (the likes of Stagecoach, Monte Rosso and Morisoli). Choose between the relaxed Valley Vista Experience, a patio tasting that includes

Where winemakers dine

Our go-to for lunch is **The Charter Oak**. When you come in through those big drapes, the first thing you see is the hearth where they're grilling, and then you see the kitchen and one big, long family table and the wooden bar. It's very inviting – and not stuffy. We love everything from the bread with homemade butter to start, to the grilled avocado and the wings, which are always good because they change monthly. The menu changes often; I love the grilled trout in a really simple beurre blanc that's not too heavy; plus, the grilled mushrooms and even the garden vegetables with the soy dip, though it's an expensive dish. They serve our Mekerra and our estate Metisse Montbleau Vineyard wine and that is huge for us. But otherwise, we usually opt for Krug bubbles and Sine Qua Non – and they make a great spicy Margarita.

Cherie and Philippe Melka, Atelier Melka

Robert Biale

Biale's award-winning Petite Sirah, or the Estate Experience with a behind-the-scenes tour of the vineyard, a barrel tasting in the cellar and a cheeseboard to accompany the wines.

biale.com

Matthiasson Winery
3175 Dry Creek Road, Napa CA 94558

In 2003, farmers Jill and Steve Matthiasson quietly started a shift towards crisp, minimal-intervention wines made with natural yeasts – something that's since become something of a movement. They craft organically grown fruit into lithe and lean Cabernet Sauvignon and spicy Cabernet Franc. They also celebrate the small vineyards of Italian wine varietals still growing in the valley, home to Refosco, Tocai Friulano and Ribolla Gialla grapes. By-appointment tastings on the outdoor patio of the Mt Veeder winery overlook their Phoenix Vineyard, a site full of old Cabernet Sauvignon,

Darioush

Cabernet Franc and Merlot vines.

matthiasson.com

Darioush

4240 Silverado Trail, Napa CA 94558

Visitors will be enthralled by founder Darioush Khaledi's amazing business success story and his luxe winery modelled on a Persian temple, with its impressive gardens, fountains and fire feature. But the real treasures are the Darioush wines, from the floral Sauvignon Blanc and the estate-grown Darius II Cabernet Sauvignon to their beloved Shiraz (aka Syrah), a grape variety suggested to have its origins in Persia. All tastings, from a Signature Mezze experience to a tasting 'By Invitation Only', include Persian-inspired delicacies selected to pair with the wines.

darioush.com

Carneros

Hudson Ranch & Vineyards

5398 Sonoma Highway, Napa CA 94559

Vintners Cristina and Lee Hudson have created a distinctive and beautiful property out in Carneros that evokes a Western ranch with its wide-open pastures and copious succulents. Join them for a seated tasting on the sunny veranda, or a more in-depth Collector Experience that includes estate olive oil along with wines, from stunning Chardonnay and Cabernet Sauvignon to a Bordeaux blend called Phoenix, plus the juicy dry white Aleatico that's made from rare Black Muscat grapes.

hudsonranch.com

Hudson Ranch

Napa Valley hotels for wine lovers

Whether you're seeking restorative spa treatments, a palatial room with vineyard views, or conveniences like world-class dining just steps from your room, there's a Napa Valley hotel to fulfill your every wish.

Solage Calistoga

Visitors have flocked to the Napa Valley seeking respite and rejuvenation in nature since the 1800s. In the upper part of the valley around St Helena and Calistoga, natural mineral springs bubble from the earth.

In the 1860s, entrepreneur and consummate host Samuel Brannan completed a railroad between San Francisco and Calistoga to make it easy for guests who didn't have motor cars to make the journey to his hot springs resort. Meanwhile, the White Sulphur Springs Resort, a magnet for the well-to-do, opened in St Helena in 1852. Guests stayed in cabins tucked into the Mayacamas Mountains and spent their days taking healing baths in the sulphur-rich waters, enjoying the waterfalls, wild flowers and wild deer.

The resort was sadly lost in the 2020 Glass Fire, but it had set the template for the ideal Napa Valley vacation: a plush place to relax and reconnect with nature. Meanwhile, down-valley establishments such as The Magnolia House in Yountville were better known for their entertainment, which included gambling, wine and women (though not necessarily in that order).

Today, Napa Valley's best hotels are still focused on highlighting its natural beauty, but the entertainment is concentrated around a civilized appreciation of the region's most celebrated attraction: wine. All of the resorts and hotels on this list offer the added perk of wine experiences. With the right booking you could find yourself unwinding with a complimentary tasting at golden hour, meeting a legendary winemaker or enjoying special access to private experiences at the top Napa Valley wineries.

Calistoga

Solage Calistoga $$$
755 Silverado Trail North, Calistoga, CA 94515

A member of the Auberge Resorts Collection, Solage Calistoga evokes the past with traditional 1920s Craftsman-style cottage accommodations outfitted with luxe-modern amenities. Whether the view is of the pool or the mountains, cottages offer airy vaulted ceilings, serene neutral décor and private patios. Soak in a

The Four Seasons Napa Valley

bath in front of the fireplace in the King Studio or choose the Silverado Suite with separate living rooms and a hot tub for two on the terrace. Poolside Picobar offers light bites and mountain views, while Solbar sees Chef Gustavo Rios specializing in California cuisine with the freshest seasonal ingredients. Thanks to the hotel's impeccable connections, guests can enjoy complimentary tastings at partner wineries including Faust, Ballentine, Darioush and Alpha Omega. Solage doesn't sleep on spa offerings either, with five geothermal pools and a detoxifying mineral mud bath to leave guests feeling brand new.

aubergeresorts.com/solage

The Four Seasons Napa Valley Resort & Residences $$$$

400 Silverado Trail, Calistoga CA 94515

Instead of a large building, The Four Seasons Napa Valley spreads itself across a series of townhouses perfectly integrated into the surrounding hills. Guests might feel like wine country denizens as they settle into their chic dwellings decorated in striking black-and-white tones, with natural wood and equestrian accents, a nod to the Silverado Trail's ranching roots. The Japanese-inspired soaking tub is the focal point of the expansive bath suite, which has a long vanity stocked with Le Labo toiletries. Along with complimentary nibbles, the minibar is stocked with everything from kombucha to Kistler Chardonnay and Cabernet Sauvignon by Elusa, the on-site winery helmed by Thomas Rivers Brown and Jonathan Walden. Drop into the casual Truss restaurant for a burger and a glass of wine, but don't miss out on the Michelin-starred degustation menus at Auro. Chef Rogelio Garcia's menu features seasonal ingredients with Japanese and Latin flavours.

fourseasons.com/napavalley

St Helena

Harvest Inn $$
1 Main St. St Helena CA 94574

This charming inn ringed by vineyards is set within 3.2 hectares of gorgeous gardens and redwood trees. Though the original inn dates back to 1975, a major renovation has since seen rooms upgraded and the lobby refreshed with a smart bar and sofas. Each room comes with a complimentary bottle of red wine from Leonardini Whitehall Lane, the family-owned winery next door. Harvest rooms include queen-size beds and soft robes, or upgrade to a Vineyard View suite for the chance to luxuriate in a private hot tub while gazing at the Leonardini vines. Guests can enjoy gratis tastings at partner wineries including Hall Wines, Freemark Abbey, Turnbull and V. Sattui. It's also worth noting that parking is complimentary, given that the hotel partners with a rental service affording access to Lincoln, Porsche, Rivian, Maserati and Jaguar vehicles.

harvestinn.com

Wydown Hotel $$
1424 Main St. St Helena, CA 94574

Wydown Hotel feels like staying at the home of a friend, albeit one with eclectic and exceptional taste in art, furnishings and décor. Local hotelier Mark Hoffmeister personally curated the public lounging spaces and 12 guest rooms in this circa-1886

building to create a modern wine country stay. Think king-size beds, large flatscreen TVs, Nespresso machines and Geneva sound systems. In the mood to get physical? Stroll down to Health Spa Napa Valley with your guest pass. Besides breakfast, guests are treated to night caps, afternoon tea and freshly baked cookies. Take advantage of hosted Friday wine tastings and discounted visits to winery partners including Cakebread, Grgich Hills, Honig, Salvestrin, Spence Vineyards, Schweiger and Titus.

wydownhotel.com

Meadowood Napa Valley $$$$

900 Meadowood Lane
St. Helena, CA 94574

When Meadowood opened in 1961, it was one of the valley's original cottage-style resorts. Bill Harlan (of Harlan Estate) bought the ailing resort in 1979, determined to make it the finest luxury resort in the USA. Guest cottages at Meadowood are expansive and yet designed with cosy nooks that invite relaxation. Turning on the fireplace and getting comfy on the sofa, curling up in the window seat with a book or slipping into the deep tub and letting stress float away are equally appealing options. There's plenty to do outside the room: tennis, hiking, golf, indulgent spa treatments or exploring a favourite varietal at a wine education centre that's exclusive to guests. Kelli A. White, the centre's education director and an esteemed wine historian and author, is as approachable as she is knowledgeable. The Forum restaurant offers breakfast, lunch and dinner, as well as a quiet spot for an expertly prepared cocktail and conversation. The concierge team can also create curated wine tour itineraries for each guest.

meadowood.com

Rutherford

Auberge du Soleil $$$$

180 Rutherford Hill Road,
Rutherford, CA 94573

Born in Algeria and raised in France, founder Claude Rouas never intended to become a hotelier, but guests at his exquisite French-Mediterranean restaurant wanted a place to stay and he obliged. When

Meadowood

Auberge du Soleil

guests drive up the hill leading to Auberge du Soleil and finally arrive at the glorious resort, there's no doubt they're in for a special experience. The auberge is a collection of 50 private rooms, suites and standalone maisons, all filled with sumptuous furnishings, linens and décor to evoke a luxe estate in Provence. No detail is overlooked, down to aligning the fountains at the spa with the views of Mount Veeder in the distance. Guests are welcomed with a splash of Cabernet Sauvignon, bubbles or rosé and during warm weather from May to August, complimentary wine tastings can be enjoyed in the courtyard. Bathing aficionados will want first dibs on a garden suite with an outdoor soaking tub.

aubergeresorts.com
aubergedusoleil

Maison Fleurie B&B $$$
6529 Yount St. Yountville CA 94599

Guests who spend the night at Maison Fleurie may feel like they've landed at an estate in the French countryside, especially when taking a stroll around the manicured paths and gardens. Perhaps it's a good thing the walls can't talk: this was once

Maison Fleurie

the site of The Magnolia House, a popular hotel circa 1873 that was rumoured to be a bordello. These days, the maison is all about peaceful repose in one of the dozen rooms appointed with fireplaces, antiques, terraces and toile de jouy textiles, or perhaps a dip in the tiled outdoor hot tub hidden behind vine-covered walls. Guests can enjoy a complimentary wine-and-cheese happy hour every evening, as well as 50% off any wine bottle purchases.

maisonfleurienapa.com

Bardessono Hotel and Spa $$$

6526 Yount St., Yountville CA 94559

Bardessono and Spa is the quintessence of zen, a certified sustainable temple of understated luxury. The name is a tribute to the family who once grew plums and walnuts here; the hotel maintains its connection to nature with its Japanese gardens and the Lucy restaurant, which sources herbs from its own kitchen garden. Biophilic rooms invite nature in with floor-to-ceiling windows, private courtyards, fireplaces and al fresco showers. A $1.65 million refresh in early 2024 saw rooms upgraded with decorative brushwork above the beds inspired by Japanese calligraphy, plus custom-made seating and stone surfaces. Bath suites are large enough for in-room spa treatments (like the grape seed scrub). But it's the gracious service that will make this a favourite Napa Valley

Bardessono Hotel and Spa

The Setting Inn

stay. Guests are greeted with a cheese plate and their wine of choice. The best wine amenity, though, is a private one-to-one on-site tasting of Heitz Martha's Vineyard with Erik Elliott, the Master Sommelier who runs the iconic cellar.

bardessono.com

The Setting Inn $$

6529 Yount St. Yountville CA 94599

This boutique inn, set in a historic 1901 farmhouse, offers a blank slate for whatever kind of experiences guests desire. If a romantic just-the-two-of-us weekend is in order, then guests will be perfectly content in spacious, traditionally designed suites with plush beds, soaking tubs, fireplaces and terraces with mountain views. Meanwhile, a self-contained cottage with two bedrooms and a pair of baths makes an ideal set-up for a family with children, couples travelling together or a getaway with the girlfriends – who can come together in the Barn, a rec room with plush seating, games and a guitar. Morning brings pastries from Thomas Keller's Bouchon Bakery and coffee from Napa Valley Coffee Roasting Company. The Setting Inn also owns a winery that specializes in Bordeaux blends and Sauvignon Blanc made by winemaker Jesse Katz of Aperture Cellars. Schedule a tasting on-site or take the scenic hour journey to Healdsburg where the wines are actually made.

thesettinginn.com

Yountville

Poetry Inn $$$$

6380 Silverado Trail, Napa, CA 94558

The Poetry Inn's speciality is an intimate stay with personalised service. Originally built by vintner Cliff Lede, the inn takes its name from his nearby Poetry Vineyard. It features just five suites named after American poets and with individualized décor, although each features stunning valley views, heated bathroom floors, and blush-coloured marble surrounding the bathtubs. The Emily Dickinson is a serene space in blue and white with natural accents,

Where winemakers dine

We like **Goose & Gander** in St Helena – it's so cute. It's very well known for its incredible cocktail programme, but the wine list is the secret, cool part of the menu because they have an unbelievable selection of local wines. They tend to get stuff that is hard for other people to get hold of because they have such good relationships with winemakers.

It's an old craftsman property with a homey feel and a beautiful outdoor courtyard. I am more of a veggie – they grow vegetables for the menu – so I go for their amazing grilled cauliflower dish but there is always perfectly cooked fish, great salads and an excellent burger. Downstairs is a classic old cosy bar with a fireplace. It's a pretty awesome place: it just feels like you're getting a really good home-cooked meal.

**Annie Favia-Erickson,
Favia Wines**

Poetry Inn

while the Robert Frost suite, decorated in tones of charcoal and sand, offers two terraces including one with a suspended daybed that's ideal for afternoon napping. Guests can enjoy complimentary wine upon arrival and by-appointment tasting experiences at sister property Sullivan Rutherford Estate, which specializes in Merlot and Cabernet Sauvignon. Wine- or Tequila-pairing dinners can be arranged with private chef Jim Leiken for an additional charge.

poetryinn.com

Napa City

Archer Hotel $$
1230 First St. Napa CA 94559

Staying at the Archer Hotel puts guests in the heart of all the action in Napa, which is currently the most vibrant city

Archer Hotel

in the valley. You're steps from scores of great restaurants, shops, more than 60 wine tasting rooms and scenic attractions such as kayaking on the Napa River. The Archer has six different room types, including suites with balconies. The best amenities are outside the room, though. Head to the rooftop spa for a hot stone massage or visit Sky & Vine Rooftop Bar to enjoy lobster corn dogs and Margherita pizza. Don't miss cuisine curated by American celebrity chef Charlie Palmer at his eponymous steakhouse. Guests can also enjoy complimentary tastings at the Vintner's Collective, a downtown tasting room, or redeem discounted tastings at wineries including Merryvale, Ballentine, Jessup Cellars, Cakebread, Rutherford Ranch and Cliff Lede Vineyards. Alternatively, choose from more than 100 special bottlings at the hotel's Whisky Bar.

archerhotel.com/napa

The McClelland House B&B $$$
569 Randolph St. Napa, CA 94559

Stepping inside the McClelland House, you feel the thrill of what it must have been like to live in a stately Victorian mansion. Originally built in 1879, Napa Valley's first woman doctor once called this landmark residence her home. Historic features including the stained-glass door, sweeping front staircase and tiled fireplaces have been lovingly restored. Current owner Choolwe Kalulu has worked with a designer to add harmonious modern décor and features to each of the five suites. A favourite is the Bond Suite, with a starburst chandelier, pale-

McClelland House

blue ceiling and plush orange velvet slipper chairs inspired by a vintage Hermès scarf. Guests enjoy a welcome wine service with their choice of red, white or sparkling wine, plus a nightly wine-and-cheese happy hour and full hot breakfast cooked to order and served in the grand dining room.

themcclellandhouse.com

Senza Hotel $$$

4066 Howard Lane, Napa CA 94558

If you like a balance between serenity and being close enough to the action, the Senza Hotel is an ideal choice. Guests drawn to relaxation can take a dip in the pool, stroll in the rose garden or book a spa treatment featuring local grape seeds. Yet the hotel is steps from Bistro Don Giovanni and Ashes & Diamonds Winery is just a short drive away. Guest rooms, which are spread among a handful of grey wood buildings, feature understated décor with colourful accents. Couples can curl up in a Senza Suite with a loft bedroom, while families may prefer a Queen Suite that accommodates four overnight guests. All rooms feature good natural light, fireplaces and espresso machines. Stop by the hotel's Library Cafe from 6 to 7pm most evenings for complimentary tastings by wine brands including Venge Vineyards, James Cole and Bella Union.

senzahotel.com

Carneros

Carneros Resort and Spa $$$$

4048 Sonoma Highway Napa, CA 94559

With its expansive vineyards, open fields and inlets ringed by fog-shrouded mountains, the

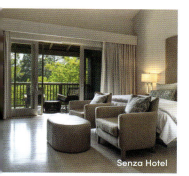
Senza Hotel

Carneros Resort and Spa feels a world away from the rest of the Napa Valley. In past eras, the picturesque landscape was once grazing land for dairy cows and sheep that lend the region its name (carneros means 'the rams' in Spanish). Farmhouse-chic guest cottages decorated in soothing colour palettes feature bedrooms that open onto a private back terrace with fire pits and chaise longues. Groups travelling with friends or children will want to consider a two-cottage suite with a shared living space and patio. Elevated amenities in Harvest Cottages include beds with sleep-enhancing technology (pressure relief sensors adjust to prevent you from waking) and soaking tubs on the terrace, while all guests can enjoy complimentary daily wine tastings and transport to wineries within an 8km radius.

carnerosresort.com

Carneros Resort and Spa

Fine dining in Napa Valley

For all its hallowed vineyards and million-dollar wineries the Napa Valley is, at its core, a farming community. Granted, it's a posh one, but the people who keep this region humming are focused on nurturing vines and soil, crushing grapes and getting their hands dirty. Perhaps that explains why many of Napa Valley's best restaurants tend to be on the casual side, designed for people with refined tastes who also happen to dine in flannel and work boots, and with grape-stained hands.

Auro, Calistoga

Undoubtedly, the biggest influence on Napa Valley's fine dining scene has been Chef Thomas Keller's iteration of the French Laundry, which debuted in 1994 with tasting menus in a rarefied setting. At Sally Schmitt's original French Laundry, founded in 1978, her prix fixe menu might have included lamb shanks with green garlic and mint, pork with cider and apples, mushroom soup and chocolate soufflé with sherry sauce. Keller elevated the experience inside this circa-1900 stone cottage, originally a saloon and once home to a French steam laundry, with precision cookery and impeccable service.

Even before Keller arrived, though, Napa Valley offered some scintillating haute cuisine. It debuted in 1977 at Domaine Chandon's own restaurant and hit its crescendo in 1981 with the arrival of a pair of fine-dining icons: Claude Rouas's The Restaurant at Auberge du Soleil and Bill Harlan's Restaurant at Meadowood. Thanks to chef Christopher Kostow and his team, the latter became a three-star Michelin restaurant in 2010.

'Whether the setting is minimal, rustic-chic or even Rococo, there's an air of excitement about delighting guests with the best delicacies that California's sunny climate can produce'

Though the restaurant names of today's Napa Valley are certainly much more inventive, the ethos hasn't changed. Whether the setting is minimal, rustic-chic or even Rococo, there's an air of excitement about delighting guests with the best delicacies that California's sunny climate can produce. Napa Valley's best fine-dining experiences are built around superb wine and fresh ingredients that are expertly prepared and served with grace.

Where winemakers dine

If I'm on my own, just working down Valley, I go to **Rutherford Grill**, sit at the bar and get one of their amazing salads. The flying tuna platter is my favourite: seared ahi on a salad with mango and orange and just a delicious, delicious dressing. It's a really good Asian-inspired lunch. They're also known for their grilled artichokes, which are very famous around the valley. Often I'll see a lot of locals at the bar, other vineyard managers and winemakers; it's really fun. They don't take reservations; you just show up and it's first come, first served. For dinner, I really like **The Calistoga Inn**. It has an incredible outdoor patio right along the Napa River, so the ambience is great. The outdoor bar area is very festive; it has a fire pit and a great cocktail menu. They serve a delicious paella; I can hardly go there without ordering it.

Heidi Barrett, La Sirena and Barrett and Barrett

Auro

Calistoga

Auro $$$
400 Silverado Trail North, Calistoga

Chef Rogelio Garcia has a magical way of taking familiar ingredients and transforming them with innovative preparation and striking presentation on custom-made ceramics. Perhaps that's why Auro received its first Michelin star just eight months after opening. The dégustation menu changes with the seasons, but signatures include Japanese hiramasa (yellowtail amberjack) in spicy aguachile, 50-day aged Australian Wagyu and a sweet amuse bouche served inside the enigmatic shell of an egg. The wine list is littered with icons from the likes of DRC and Château Palmer, as well as rare

Press $$$

587 St Helena Highway
S. Helena

Owned by the family behind Rudd winery, Press has become something of a gathering place for the wine industry; one where guests can enjoy a multi-course meal or simply knock back the cocktails. The likes of wagyu beef tartare, black truffle fries and a glass of Cabernet can all be enjoyed at the bar. Chef Philip Tessier and his team delight in pushing the boundaries of the classic steakhouse menu to include fanciful deconstructed seafood towers, housemade pretzels with cultured butter and caviar, surprisingly light ricotta gnudi and playful desserts that capture the season. The wine list is laser-focused on the Valley, and with 2,700 selections it

wines from boutique California producers, including expressive Shibumi Knoll Pinot Noir and Futo Estate's floral and vibrant Sauvignon Blanc (only poured here), which take the experience to another level.

auronapavalley.com

Press

The Charter Oak

makes for the most extensive collection of Napa Valley wines in the world.

pressnapavalley.com

The Charter Oak $$$
1050 Charter Oak Ave, St Helena

The Charter Oak, overseen by chef Christopher Kostow, who earned three Michelin stars just down the road at sister property Meadowood, is the quintessential Napa Valley insider's spot. Lunch is busy, and things heat up again at happy hour with a burger that some call the best in the Valley. Dinner showcases the stellar wine list plus impeccable chops, roasts and steaks, but the secret stars are the seasonal vegetable sides grown on the restaurant's farm, such as the crudités with soy dip. Wintertime brings courtyard dining in yurts while summer means slushies with Space Age rosé.

thecharteroak.com

The French Laundry $$$$
6640 Washington St, Yountville

Thomas Keller's flagship restaurant, still going strong after 30 years, has had a profound impact on fine dining around the world. Signature oysters and pearls (caviar) give way to an ever-changing cascade of courses. Recent dishes include vapour-cooked Atlantic snapper with chanterelles, and sweetbreads with choucroute butter and quail egg. The wine list is as strong on Burgundy,

Bordeaux and the other great regions as it is on Napa Valley, Sonoma and Oregon; there's also a decent by-the-glass and half-bottle offering.

thomaskeller.com/tfl

Lucy Restaurant & Bar
$$$
6526 Yount St, Yountville

The Bardessono hotel's understated luxury extends to Lucy, an on-site fine-dining restaurant. Chef Rick Edge has a deft touch with seasonal cuisine (this is California, after all) but his menu is infused with international flavours. Tuck into creamy winter squash, carrot and sweet potato soup spiced with lemongrass and ginger, meaty beef short ribs with celery root purée, and a banana split with three kinds of gelato. The wine list is littered

Lucy Restaurant & Bar

with gems, including Jeff Ames' Anthem Cabernet Sauvignon by the glass and a Burgundian Burgess Chardonnay that's made exclusively for Bardessono.

lucyyountville.com

RH Restaurant at RH Yountville $$$
6725 Washington St, Yountville

At first blush, RH Restaurant might seem to be all about the scene and the scenery. After all, where else can one nibble on Chinese chicken salad while sitting among Italianate fountains and gnarled olive trees festooned with crystal chandeliers? The menu offers classics like a whole grilled branzino (sea bass), seared ribeye steak or a burger, but the real draw are the entrée-sized salads, like the restaurant's take on a Cobb and the Mulholland Drive (named for the LA address, not David Lynch's surrealist film noir) with grilled chicken, egg, beetroot, tomato, cheddar, smoked bacon and avocado. Give

The French Laundry

Where winemakers dine

Cook is a neighbourhood restaurant; it's intimate and the owners – chef Jude and his wife, Meagan – care deeply about their customers, their employees, and, for sure, the food. I aspire to make my wines like Jude cooks, always looking for ways in which to subtly improve the quality, the artistic expression and the overall enjoyment.

The restaurant has just passed the 20-year mark in the same spot. Whether you're sitting at a table or the counter, you feel not just comfortable but loved, like there is nowhere else you'd rather be.

I like to start with a Negroni, then move onto a Chianti or a local wine that you're not likely to see elsewhere around town. I really try to mix it up, but I often fall back on the house burrata, the chopped salad, the heavenly cavatelli (all pastas are hand-rolled every day – it would have made my Italian grandmother cry), and finish up with the panna cotta.

**Chris Phelps,
AD VIVUM and Coil Wines**

RH Restaurant

in to the temptation of crispy artichokes with lemon aioli or buttery lobster rolls topped with Petrossian caviar. The wine list is strong on California, but with an interesting selection from Bordeaux, Spain, Argentina and the rest of the world.
rh.com/us/en/yountville/restaurant

Napa

Cole's Chop House $$$
1122 Main St. Napa

It's easy to see why Cole's Chop House is hailed as one of the best steakhouses in America. The selection of 21-day dry-aged

steaks and chops is dazzling, but they're only part of Cole's popularity. The real secret is the warm, expert service. Standout dishes include crostini with mushrooms in a veal reduction, oysters Rockefeller, bacon blue cheese wedge salad and cauliflower with capers, garlic and chilli flakes. The wine list offers near-impossible-to-find bottles from producers including Colgin, Bryant Family, Hundred Acre, Joseph Phelps and Ghost Horse. Equally impressive are the clever dessert pairings: think banana cream pie with Inniskillin Vidal Icewine.

coleschophouse.com

Cole's Chop House

Angèle Restaurant & Bar

Angèle Restaurant & Bar
$$$
540 Main St. Napa

Gracious hospitality comes naturally to Bettina Rouas, daughter of Claude, the founder of The Restaurant at Auberge du Soleil. She followed in his footsteps working front of house at French Laundry and French-Italian Florio in San Francisco, before opening Angèle. Tucked away in a historic boathouse overlooking the Napa River, this bustling bistro lovingly recreates all the French classics: from oysters with Champagne mignonette and hearty salad lyonnaise with lentils and bacon, to duck confit and beef bourguignon. Handmade Italian pastas are also a speciality, only surpassed by the Franco-American wine list that visits all the right regions, from the Rhône to the Russian River Valley with lots of Napa Valley icon wines included along the way. Angèle is a go-to for winemakers and Napa visitors alike, who are seduced by the thought of spending a couple of hours on the sun-warmed patio.

angelerestaurant.com

Bear at Stanly Ranch $$
200 Stanly Crossroad, Napa

The focal point of the new restaurant at Stanly Ranch resort is the open kitchen where chef Garrison Price employs live-fire cooking. Start with the bison tartare with fermented chillies and a rice cracker flourish, or ephemeral maitake mushroom tempura. Standout entrées include the fire-roasted lamb ribs with spices that change seasonally, and whole rainbow trout from Mt Lassen. On a sunny day, children can play lawn games while parents linger over desserts such as sourdough ice cream with umami-rich yeast caramel, and apple pie served as a trifle. Complimentary valet parking is another treat.

aubergeresorts.com/stanlyranch

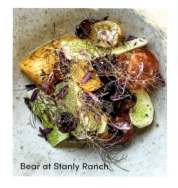
Bear at Stanly Ranch

Kenzo Restaurant $$$
1339 Pearl St. Napa

Before she and her husband Kenzo opened their Napa dining room, Natsuko Tsujimoto ran the couple's four haute cuisine Kenzo restaurants in Japan. Here in Napa, they also own Kenzo Estate Winery, with this downtown restaurant as a sister property. The discreet Michelin-starred space offers kaiseki ryori, the ultimate in seasonally inspired cuisine. Chef Kenzo Miyaishi creates multi-course menus that feature the crème de la crème of local produce plus seafood and fin fish specialities flown in from Toyosu Market in Tokyo. While the restaurant has an extensive international wine and sake list, winemaker Marc Nanes crafts Kenzo's wines, from Asatsuyu Sauvignon Blanc to Ai Cabernet Sauvignon, to pair with Japanese cuisine.

kenzonapa.com

Kenzo

Napa Valley wine shops

Whether you're on the hunt for rare cult California classics, bottles from the region's undiscovered producers or an international experience while on the wine trail, these Napa Valley wine shops are where the locals – sommeliers and winemakers included – go to buy their wine.

Decant Bottle Shop & Bar

Despite global economic challenges and declining wine consumption, Napa Valley continues to thrive. Thanks to its haute-living appeal and a relentless pursuit of excellence, the region has remained in the American fine wine winner's circle. Once its wines achieved cult status among collectors, Napa Valley never let up; today, its best bottles rival Burgundy and Bordeaux in terms of quality, price and exclusivity. As such, Napa Valley is home to some of the finest wine shops in the country – even its local Costco recently made headlines when it launched with what the retailer claims to be its largest wine selection nationwide, and which reportedly boasts bottles of anything from Shafer and Heitz to Lafite Rothschild and Haut-Brion within its offering.

'There's a real savvy to staff behind the counter... ask as many questions as you can and you'll be in line for an impromptu education'

Away from the supermarkets, Napa Valley's best wine boutiques are as much about the in-store experience as they are about the purchases. There's a real savvy to staff behind the counter, often keen to impart the histories of the wines in stock. Ask as many questions as you can and you'll be in line for an impromptu education. The shelves are lined with eye candy for Napa Valley enthusiasts, but they are also home to the smaller jewels of Napa Valley that don't have as wide a distribution or the same connections to big retail.

For those in the know, it's easy to max out both luggage space and budgets when in the Valley. So where should you shop to ensure your money and time are well spent? Go where the wine pros go. Here's a guide to where Napa Valley insiders buy their wine – some of the region's most compelling wine shops, and by extension, among the best in the world.

Where winemakers dine

Angèle owner Bettina Rouas can often be seen on the dining room floor making sure clients are being well taken care of. Angèle explores the bounty of Northern California through the lens of French country cuisine. You will often find locals, winemakers and tourists 'in the know', exploring the well-thought-out wine list and taking in the friendly vibes. Whether you are having duck confit, beef bourguignon or a classic burger, your palate will be met with delicious and familiar flavours.

Artie Johnson, Le Artishasic

Acme Fine Wines

St Helena

ACME Fine Wines
1118 Hunt Ave, St Helena, CA 94574

This women-owned-and-operated boutique has been a cornerstone of Napa Valley's wine scene for over two decades. Founded by Karen Williams, who moved to Napa Valley in 1998 to immerse herself in the wine industry, ACME specializes in discovering and launching inaugural releases from emerging Napa Valley brands, many of which are exclusive to the shop. Among them, you'll find Summer Dreams by Jayson Woodbridge of Hundred

selection of highly allocated, iconic wines from both classic producers and under-the-radar makers and from various wine-growing regions worldwide, although the focus is on local Napa Valley creations. The dynamic team of sommeliers provides a personalised service, tailoring selections to individual preferences and budgets. ACME also offers curated tasting experiences, daily email offerings with exclusive releases, and wine club memberships that focus on undiscovered wines of the highest quality. The shop is open to the public by appointment or by chance: calling ahead is advised.

acmefinewines.com

Acre and Nid Tissé, a very tiny production wine from Marie-Laure Ammons, who worked for 18 years at wine consultancy Atelier Melka. The gallery-style setting offers a curated

Oakville

Oakville Grocery
7856 St Helena Hwy, Oakville

Oakville Grocery has been a

Oakville Grocery

staple of the area since 1881 and remains a must-visit while in Napa Valley. Now owned by Jean-Charles Boisset, this historic shop is a true institution and one of the region's most photographed landmarks. While its artisanal fresh fare is its modern claim to fame, the wine selection is equally impressive – a who's who of Napa Valley's top producers, filled with icon wines and exciting discoveries for both collectors and casual drinkers alike. Inside the shop, the Wine Vault boasts an exceptional selection of both local and imported wines, from Krug Champagne to JCB sparkling wines and sought-after Burgundy selections. Frequent events, including live music nights, add to the charm, making Oakville Grocery not just a stop for provisions but a lively community hub. For those looking to explore even more, the adjacent Oakville Wine Merchant & History Museum offers insight into Napa Valley's rich viticultural past.

oakvillegrocery.com

Yountville

V Wine Cellar

6525 Washington St, Yountville, CA 94599

This cosy yet sophisticated shop in Yountville has been affectionately dubbed 'Napa Valley's Living Room'. Founded nearly two decades ago, it is led by Larry 'Shup' Shupnick, a hospitality veteran with six decades of experience, and Scott Lewis, a former hotel food and beverage professional. While the shop offers plenty of local staples, what sets it apart is its ability to secure stunning, hard-to-find releases from Napa Valley and beyond, making it

K. Laz Wine Collection

a favourite among local wine pros. V Wine Cellar also provides concierge and cellar appraisal services, hosts private receptions and features an outdoor cigar patio – a rare luxury for Napa Valley's wine scene.

winecellar.com

K. Laz Wine Collection
6484 Washington St suite c, Yountville

A high-end tasting destination in Yountville, K. Laz Wine Collection was founded by wine industry insider Kerrin Laz, former wine director for the renowned California grocer Dean & DeLuca. Laz's portfolio showcases her remarkable ability to acquire some of the most sought-after wines in the region, including bottles that command five-figure price tags (think Screaming Eagle, Harlan, Futo, Realm, Hundred Acre, Bryant Family, Abreu and Dalla Valle). Beyond Napa, the selection extends to standout Champagnes, often served by the glass and paired with exquisite caviar in-store. Despite its elite offerings, K. Laz maintains a welcoming atmosphere, avoiding any overt sense of exclusivity. The space is designed for browsing, sipping and private tastings, making it a go-to destination for collectors and enthusiasts.

klazwinecollection.com

Honor Market
6795 Washington St, Yountville, CA 94599

Honor Market easily takes the spot as the most fun shop on this list. Don't let its simple

yet charming façade fool you – at this well-appointed quick stop, you can fill up your tank while also filling up your wine basket. This combination grocer and petrol station houses an impressive wine selection to complement the array of local delicacies stocked within its old-school Napa Valley walls. Think hard-to-obtain bottles from the likes of Farella, Groth Vineyards, Royal Prince (made by Maayan Koschitsky of Atelier Melka), Paul Hobb's Crossbarn Winery, Textbook, Paradigm and Flowers. It offers a great chance to pick up something absolutely delicious at a very fair price to be enjoyed back at your hotel room or over dinner. And while waiting on the petrol, there's no better way to pass the time than with Honor's excellent coffee and pastry selection.

instagram.com/
honormarketyountville

Napa

Compline Wine Shop
1300 First St. #319
Downtown Napa, CA 94559

Associated with the restaurant of the same name – lauded as one of America's Top 100 Wine Restaurants less than a year after opening – Compline's urban yet upscale wine shop on Napa's First Street has become a go-to for the region's wine pros. The carefully curated selection is nothing short of spectacular, offering a jaw-dropping array of French, Italian and Spanish wines plus Champagne labels ranging from iconic producers to sommelier secret weapons. The California section alone

is a veritable who's who of the state's top wineries, while additional selections include excellent port and sherry as well as an impressive lineup of large-format bottles for those looking to splurge. Compline also regularly hosts winemaker-led tasting events and talks, often featuring well-known names (recent examples include Dan Petroski of Massican among the locals, and from further afield, makers of the likes of Jean-Louis Chave and Gravner). The shop itself is brightly lit and inviting, designed for both browsing and lingering. A comfortable front room allows guests to sit and enjoy wines by the glass

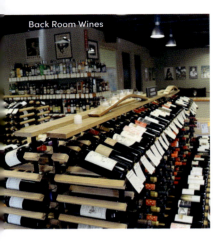

or bottle, for those keen to explore before committing to a purchase. Compline also offers the option to purchase a bottle to drink directly in its sister restaurant, just metres from the shop's front door.

complinewine.com/collections

Back Room Wines
1000 Main St STE 120, Napa, CA 94559

Back Room Wines has become a (quite justifiably) famous destination for wine shopping in Napa Valley, having been in business for nearly a quarter of a century. Specializing in collectable, rare and limited-edition wines – not just from Napa Valley, but worldwide – the shop currently boasts an inventory of more than 800 bottles from 14 different countries. Hard-to-find local gems from names such as Paloma, Kongsgaard and O'Shaughnessy are often in stock, alongside an impressive selection of spirits. Those seeking something truly special should peruse the 'Rare & Collectible' section, where it's all too easy to part with a significant sum for a coveted bottle. The shop's intimate and unpretentious setting is a refreshing contrast to some of the valley's grander winery tasting rooms, offering a welcoming, no-frills environment where wine lovers can browse at leisure or seek expert guidance from the knowledgeable staff.

backroomwines.com

Maison Fayard
1408 2nd St, Napa, CA 94559

Featuring only wines made by renowned winemaker Julien Fayard, stepping into Maison Fayard on Downtown Napa's Second Street feels like entering a luxurious, sophisticated wine retreat. While it functions as a tasting room, it's designed more like an impeccably curated wine shop – beautifully lit with handsome chandeliers made from wooden staves that call to mind a deconstructed wine barrel. High ceilings give the feeling of being in a classic library; one where the 'bookshelves' display eye-catching labels instead of the spines of classic novels. While it offers a rare opportunity to explore Fayard's highly sought-after wines in one place, the brands Fayard works with are the stuff of Napa Valley legend – including Somnium, Covert, Sire and Mithra – and often otherwise difficult to obtain. In this elegant, intimate setting, guests can not only taste and purchase bottles but can also find a selection of high-end wine accessories to complement their selections.

maisonfayard.com

Outer Space Wines
974 Franklin St, Napa, CA 94559

Restaurateurs Thad and Emily Duprey purchased Outer Space Wines from Napa wine

Maison Fayard

Thad and Emily Duprey of Outer Space Wines

professional Dan Dawson – the inaugural sommelier at Thomas Keller's renowned The French Laundry in Yountville – in August 2024. Located in Downtown Napa, this kitschy yet engaging tasting room and event space may appear whimsical with its astro-themed décor, but the selection is taken very seriously. The inventory is thoughtfully divided, with approximately half dedicated to Northern Californian wines and the other half to carefully curated European selections, including rare sparkling and dessert wines from small producers. The wine bar offers daily tastings of local wines, as well as special events (typically later in the week). Cheese plates and wine-friendly snacks are available at all times to complement the wine – and the shop also hosts food-and-wine pairing events on Thursdays and Fridays.

outerspacewines.com

Decant Bottle Shop & Bar

2999 Solano Ave, Napa, CA 94558

Sommeliers Cara Patricia and Simi Grewal founded Decant in San Francisco's SoMa neighbourhood and in 2024 expanded into Napa with a wine shop located at 2999 Solano Avenue. Decant specializes in off-the-beaten-path wines sourced exclusively from sustainably farmed vineyards. The shop's 'School of Decant' classes explore wine regions and growing concepts through comparative tastings.

The shop organizes its selection from a fresh perspective, highlighting women-owned, BIPOC-owned and LGBTQ-made brands. In addition to wines, Decant offers cheese, tinned seafood, beer, cider and various bottle formats, from small to large. The Napa location also features a bar area where patrons can enjoy wines by the glass or bottle in a truly welcoming atmosphere.

decantnapa.com

Gillian Ballance MS, Simi Grewal and Cara Patricia of Decant Bottle Shop & Bar

Napa Valley wineries with great food

Food and wine were made for each other – and no one knows that better than the Valley's clutch of gourmet winemakers, whose mouthwatering food pairings match their craft in the winery with their skills in the kitchen.

Darioush

Even if it's possible to live on wine and cheese alone, one probably shouldn't, especially while travelling in wine country and (over)indulging on a near-constant basis. But while many wine regions around the world have estates that feature full-on restaurants in the grounds, this concept isn't as popular in Napa Valley, which has local beverage laws that complicate matters. Luckily, many wineries have discovered that a little culinary creativity goes a long way. Napa Valley's fabled estates have developed increasingly exciting and robust food-and-wine pairing options to offer to visitors, the likes of which make a simple cheese plate seem downright passé.

'Napa Valley's fabled estates have developed exciting and robust food and wine pairings'

From private chefs offering tasting menus that could rival any Michelin-starred restaurant to pairing plates drawing from estate gardens and their bounty of seasonal produce, these wineries have pulled out all the stops to create food-and-wine experiences that visitors will remember for a lifetime. While some of these offerings may be a bit spendy, you might find something revelatory in a carefully crafted pairing; when done well, these combinations can elevate both the food and the wine beyond their individual excellence, helping highlight flavour nuances that may have previously been hidden.

It would probably be overkill to book too many of these types of food-and-wine pairings in one day, but if you schedule them thoughtfully you may not need to seek out a lunch reservation – therefore maximizing on time spent exploring some of the world's most renowned wineries. From Los Carneros at the southern end of the region to Calistoga all the way up north, here are some leading wineries where you can taste, unwind and fill up in Napa Valley.

Davis Estates

Davis Estates
4060 Silverado Trail N, Calistoga, CA 94515

'The goal of the food pairing is to change the conversation with the guest. What better way to really have a back-and-forth conversation?' says Jessica Link, president of Davis Estates. Link's point is well made. Experimenting with how food and wine can interact is a fantastic – and indulgent – way in for customers. Davis Estates puts an emphasis on punchy and compelling flavours, using a coconut and red lentil soup with spinach, cilantro, Aleppo pepper and toasted coconut to highlight its Chardonnay, and a soba noodle salad with Shimeji mushrooms, sesame dressing, cashews, edamame, furakake and tatsoi (an Asian brassica) to showcase the depths of its Merlot.

These aren't simple dishes that allow the wines to dominate; they are exciting and deliberate choices that engage with the wines at a higher level and, as intentioned, foster some deep conversations.

davisestates.com

Tamber Bey
1251 Tubbs Ln, Calistoga, CA 94515

Tamber Bey is an enchanting place to spend a leisurely afternoon, especially if you're an equestrian or animal lover. This horse farm and winery makes beautiful whites and reds and offers a range of

Tasting room, Tamber Bey

accompaniments that can be added to the tasting experience, from box lunches to hearty snack boards. But what you really need to know is that Tamber Bey offers a completely unique 'savoury cookie pairing'. Yes, you read that right. The idea is that these not-quite-sweet cookies should elevate the wines in beautiful and unexpected ways. It's a delightfully playful twist on the pairing concept.

tamberbey.com

St Helena

Wheeler Farms
588 Zinfandel Ln, St Helena, CA 94574

Winemaker Nigel Kinsman crafts a range of wines from distinctive vineyards throughout Napa Valley. From Vine Hill Ranch, Diamond Mountain, Oakville and George III, these Cabernets all carry distinct minerality and structure gained from their particular terroir. The estate offers three tasting experiences, loaded with ingredients from its own culinary garden, to pair with these exceptional wines. Chef Tom Harder serves four canapés in the simplest pairing, as well as a full-blown lunch or a chef's table option that sees Harder himself prepare the four-course menu before your eyes. Menus evolve regularly to highlight the very best of what's in season.

wheelerfarmswine.com

Joseph Phelps
200 Taplin Road. St. Helena, CA 94574

This iconic Napa Valley estate has been electrifying food and wine lovers for decades – the flagship wine, Insignia, long a favourite of chefs and sommeliers alike. Phelps has recently revitalized its visitor centre and now offers multiple culinary tasting experiences crafted by chef Tod Kawachi to pair with its legendary Napa

Wheeler Farms

Joseph Phelps

Where winemakers dine

I love **Cole's Chop House**. The owners are just very down to earth, very humble, and they go out of their way to give you a great experience. That's what we always look for wherever we go, because you can't buy that. I love the building: part of one of the original buildings in Napa.

It's a steakhouse, but there is also nice seafood, lobster tails and prawns on the menu. There's crab and halibut; they make the best oysters Rockefeller; and the steaks are amazing. My favourite is the cowboy steak, a bone-in ribeye. And then the hash browns are incredible: they're the best in the country. I like the freshness, the crunchiness of them; you know, you can't stop eating them. For dessert, they have a wonderful whiskey pudding and when they have it on the menu, the carrot cake is amazing.

Rolando Herrera, Mi Sueño

Valley wines, as well as selections from Joseph Phelps' lesser-known but equally admirable Sonoma Coast vineyards. The 'Collector's Tasting' features a small number of bites to pair with the range of wines, while more serious foodies can indulge in the 'Taste of Place' or 'Chef's Culinary Menu', with Insignia poured alongside Snake River Farm's American wagyu beef, and a Bloomsdale spinach tartlet with baby turnip and a red-wine herb jus.

josephphelps.com

Rutherford

Cakebread Cellars

8300 St Helena Hwy,
Rutherford, CA 94573

Since the early seventies, Cakebread has been a standout for Napa Valley Sauvignon Blanc and Cabernet, earning international recognition and accolades from fans and wine critics alike. The Cakebread

family knew early on that food and wine are two sides of the same coin – and great food, like great wine, starts in the dirt. Obviously, then, the experience at Cakebread begins with a tour of Dolores Cakebread's original culinary garden. Chefs Brian Streeter and Josh Anderson employ a wide range of cuisine styles to pair with Cakebread's array of vinous offerings, from Sauvignon Blanc and Chardonnay to Cabernet and Syrah. As the menu highlights the bounty of the garden, offerings evolve throughout the year, as do the accompanying wines. A seasonal pairing of four bites is offered twice daily and can be modified to allow for food allergies as needed.

cakebread.com

Round Pond Estate

875 Rutherford Rd, Rutherford, CA 94573

While many wineries plant olive trees alongside vineyards, Round Pond takes it all to the next level with its 2,200 olive trees, a mix of eight different varieties from Italy and Spain. Oil production is no simple affair either, with a combination of a modern mill and a traditional stone press that weighs thousands of pounds.

The 'Taste of the Estate' experience offers a flight of wines alongside a tasting of said olive oils and accoutrements. Those with a little more time (or a bigger appetite) can opt for the 'Il Pranzo' experience, which includes a tour of the vineyards and gardens before sitting down to a four-course menu prepared by chef Fernando Arias featuring dishes like Petrale sole with kumquat, radish and estate greens paired with Round Pond Sauvignon Blanc.

roundpond.com

Sequoia Grove

8338 St Helena Hwy, Napa, CA 94558

If you're a Cabernet purist

with an unwavering devotion to the full-bodied and hearty, you'll likely be craving a seriously elevated pairing for these serious wines. Seatings for Sequoia Grove's 'A Taste for Cabernet' experience sell out fast, a luxurious offering that features innovative and Japanese-tinged courses by executive chef Spencer Conaty. The menu invites the diner to discover 'the surprising versatility of Cabernet Sauvignon through a multi-course journey', with dishes that include wild-caught sea bass, celery root three ways, sesame gremolata and black garlic. There's even an evening version of the event, held a few Fridays per month. If you're looking for a more relaxed vibe, you can also taste Sequoia Grove's wines with a sampling of small bites.

sequoiagrove.com

Oakville

B Cellars

703 Oakville Cross Rd, Napa, CA 94558

B Cellars prides itself on the art of blending, crafting a range of unique wines that go beyond classic varietal character. To elevate the tasting experience for visitors, the Oakville estate has begun pairing wines with whimsical 'B Bites' that change with the seasons – or any time that inspiration strikes. Here, you might find Sauvignon Blanc paired with pineapple curried shrimp, or Cabernet Sauvignon with an elevated expression of pastrami on rye. One particularly exciting flavour combination is struck between Blend 25, a Cabernet/Syrah blend, and goat ravioli with carrot purée and crispy chickpea. Some bites are smaller, some more filling, but every morsel helps to bring the winery's vision for pairing food and wine into sharp focus.

bcellars.com

Oak Knoll

Darioush

4240 Silverado Trail, Napa, CA 94558

The Persian heritage of founders Darioush and Shahpar Khaledi is front and centre in a brand-new culinary programme at Darioush. Time-honoured

Darioush

techniques and ingredients mingle with seasonal produce from the garden to create a menu that enchants, while pairing marvellously with these elegant and refined wines. While all tasting experiences at Darioush involve some culinary flair, the most singular experience is entitled 'By Invitation Only' and is served in two prescheduled seatings per day. This tasting offers a chance for guests to enjoy the estate's most exclusive wines alongside immaculately presented courses, including Hokkaido scallop with sunchoke and bacon jam, designed by executive chef Sean Massey and longtime Darioush chef Juan Carlos Acosta.

darioush.com

Napa City

Gentleman Farmer
1564 1st St, Napa, CA 94559

Can't wait to get your day started? Gentleman Farmer hosts its 'Wine and a Breakfast of Champions' experience that starts with your choice of a five-kilometre jog or guided meditation before a sumptuous wine-paired breakfast. Food includes craveable bites like house-cured pancetta and brioche alongside mustard made with their own Chardonnay, salmon rillettes, personal soufflés, and a massive array of desserts. We're not sure if the jog is quite enough to burn off the sheer number of calories, but it certainly could take the edge off. The action takes place in a Downtown bungalow, but the founders make wine on a very small scale in St Helena and pour the results alongside this slap-up brunch fare. A perfect way for wine travellers to rise and shine.

gentlemanfarmerwines.com

Carneros

Domaine Carneros
1240 Duhig Rd, Napa, CA 9455

If you're looking for an opportunity to push the boat out when in wine country, look no further than Domaine

In the kitchen at Gentleman Farmer

Where winemakers dine

I love going to **Torc** in Napa. When you walk in the front door it feels like a little bit of history because you're walking in through one of those historic buildings with stone walls and wooden floors. There's a bar that people can eat at, and it feels very comfortable; you can see the chef cooking in the back of the room. There are wonderful window seats if you want to be that person in the window (we love being in the window) and they have fun booths, too. Husband-and-wife team Sean and Cynthia forage for their own mushrooms and don't tell anybody where they go. In winter they're doing black truffles on pasta, and I've enjoyed really fun plays on classic surf and turf, like lobster and tri-tip.

For dessert, I like the cookies because they go with a little bit of Tequila off their list or one of their sweet wines. They've got a dark chocolate pie and they make their own ice cream. You know, salted caramel ice cream... you just can't go wrong.

Pam Starr, Crocker & Starr

Domaine Carneros

Carneros at the southern end of Napa in the Los Carneros AVA. This elite sparkling house, which was originally launched by Champagne Taittinger in 1987, produces some of California's best sparklers and hosts guests in grand fashion at a château designed to evoke the Champagne maison. Domaine Carneros recently opened the Salon des Rêves, a swanky art deco-inspired lounge overlooking the impeccable riddling room and offering an array of decadent seafood-focused pairings, including a comparative tasting of Atlantic and Pacific oysters, caviar by

Tsar Nicoulai and a sumptuous house ceviche. The lavish green-and-gold space is accessed via a hidden staircase, giving the whole experience a mysterious, speakeasy vibe.

domainecarneros.com

The Donum Estate
24500 Ramal Road Sonoma, CA 95476

The Donum Estate, home to one of the largest outdoor sculpture parks in the world, is absolutely breathtaking. The 220 acre (90ha) estate focuses on the production of regeneratively and organically farmed Chardonnay and Pinot Noir, but also houses an olive grove, plum orchard and a culinary garden that is the source for an array of creative canapés and small plates, each paired with wines in 'Discover' and 'Explore' experiences. Donum leans all the way into an ethos of local production, even serving some items on housemade ceramics crafted from the estate's own clay. If you feel like lingering a bit, you can also choose a full-blown lunch service.

Either way, plan some extra time to enjoy the grounds and the art.

thedonumestate.com

The Donum Estate

Napa Valley wine bars

While Napa Valley's many Michelin-starred restaurants and 100-point wines attract attention, it's in the region's vibrant wine bars, owned and frequented by representatives from the local communities they serve, that visitors can make some of the most exciting vinous discoveries.

The Saint, St Helena

The best Napa Valley wine bars list some of the most interesting new and small producers from both California and abroad, all in a comfortable, convivial and lively setting.

Because it is prohibitively expensive for many small wineries to have their own, or even a collaborative, tasting room, wine bars are often used to highlight rotating flights of a single producer's wines. It wouldn't be unusual to hear one of Napa Valley's star winemakers say that 'the best place to try my wine is at such and such wine bar'. The region's wine bars are usually located in the city centres, as well; while you'll sacrifice the sprawling vineyard views of tasting rooms and resorts, you'll instead get to experience the true pulse of Napa Valley and its colourful local life over a glass of something special.

'It's not unusual to hear a star winemaker say the best place to try their wine is at such-and-such wine bar'

In a region that is home to the Culinary Institute of America and where so many sommeliers and wine professionals come to train, learn and live, you can expect thoughtful and well-curated selections – wines designed to pair perfectly with fresh, regional cuisine, whether it is a skilfully plated presentation of perfectly seared scallops, a pile of tender brisket or a wood-fired pizza with locally made buffalo mozzarella.

Compline, Napa City

You'd be encouraged to make time in between (or instead of) the elaborate wine tours or the multi-course tasting menus for these more humble, yet memorable, Napa Valley wine bar experiences.

Where winemakers dine

My go-to is **Mustards Grill** for its soulful comfort food. The wine list is incredible, and the people are great. It's where you see all the other winemakers: it's the local. We like to start with the ahi tuna tostada. Nine times out of ten I order the Mongolian pork chop, so you've got some cabbage on the side and it's the right balance of sweet and savoury. The wine list is always changing; that's the beauty of Mustards. You also get to dive deep as the list is so long. As far as cocktails go, I routinely order 'The Final Word'. It's a play on The Last Word that's made with rye and lemon juice.

Nigel Kinsman, Kinsman Eades

Calistoga

SolBar
755 Silverado Trail N

SolBar is located in the Solage hotel just outside of Calistoga at the north end of the valley. The sprawling property, which is part of the prestigious Auberge Resort Collection, is just enough off the beaten path to make it feel like a destination. Don't expect SolBar to feel like a bar tagged on to a hotel: this full-service restaurant and lounge features high ceilings, large glass doors and an expansive patio with views of the pool and surrounding vineyards. For wine, this is the place to get all the biggest names with the smallest allocations in Napa Valley, with verticals and horizontals of Aubert, Shafer, Opus One, Bond and Hundred Acre just to name (drop) a few. Be prepared to pay for the privilege, of course. But if a delightful bottle of Alsatian Riesling to pair with the seafood-centric menu is more your speed, fear not: the list has something for pretty much every palate and price point.

aubergeresorts.com/solage/dine/solbar

St Helena

The Saint
1351 Main Street

This cosy wine bar smack in the middle of St Helena, on the historic Main Street, is run by the same couple who make Night Wines – a boutique, high-end Napa Valley wine brand. So of course you can taste their Cabernet, Merlot and Chardonnay here, as well as a small and thoughtful, if fairly mainstream, selection of other local and international wines by the glass, including two Champagnes. In addition to the bar itself and some lovely sidewalk tables, the seating area is arranged living-room style for maximum comfort. The menu, organized by light bites, small, or larger plates, can be perfect for a light snack, a shared experience or a full dinner.

thesaintnapavalley.com

Erosion Tap House
1234 Main Street

This 'tap house' on Main Street in downtown St Helena has two distinct spaces: a brightly lit 'Wine Bar & Ice Cream Parlour' featuring pastel Jonathan Adler-esque furniture, and a Beer Hall offering a rotating selection of local and international brews (one of the founders is a Master Ciserone). Erosion, named for the historical soil event that shapes the geography of the Valley, also has its own wine brand, which is poured across the respective bars. So yes, there is a lot going on. But this family-owned and run establishment is all about making guests feel comfortable and ready for a good time; one of the

The Saint

Erosion Tap House

owners is almost always on the floor guiding guests through extensive options that include a food offering that reads like a kids' menu for grown-ups: think loaded tater tots, waffle pretzels and a 'Pizza Party'. The wine list is equally as playful: each section (sparkling, white, red) leads with Erosion-made wines with names like 'Unicorn Eyes' and 'Carbonara Girl' (what that tells you about the wine is up to you), before getting down to business with a handful of 'guest wineries' from near and far that are all available by the glass.

erosion.buzz

Napa City

Compline
1300 First Street #312

Since it opened in 2018 in a newly developed outdoor mall in downtown Napa, Compline (as much restaurant as wine bar) has become a favourite among the local wine community. Founded by master sommelier Matt Stamp and Charlie Trotter-trained hospitality professional Ryan Stetins, it brought one of the best wine programmes to the Valley with a Burgundy selection deep enough to appease the most discerning connoisseur as well as more obscure wines from the

Compline

likes of Santorini and the Canary Islands. As for Napa Valley look for back vintages from legends like Cathy Corison and Philip Togni, likely purchased directly from their cellars. Sophisticated and unpretentious, this is a wonderful place for a glass or flight of wines and the food is fantastic, making it a perfectly suitable option for dining (and an opportunity to delve into the extensive bottle list). In 2022, the team added a robust bottle shop of the same name just around the corner.

complinewine.com

Cadet
930 Franklin Street

Like Compline, Cadet has long been a gathering spot for local winemakers and wine lovers. The wine bar's commitment to the community is unparalleled, hosting weekly educational tastings, classes and flights. It is a place where you can nerd out during an early evening soil seminar or guided wine tasting with a local legend, then party late into the night, popping bottles of grower Champagne while the music blasts. The food options are limited to cheese and charcuterie, making it most suitable for a relaxing glass of wine before dinner or for a night cap later on, when it can get quite, er, lively. Fortunately, its location is within stumbling distance or a short taxi ride to the many hotels and Airbnbs of downtown Napa.

cadetbar.com

Bounty Hunter
975 1st Street

This 'Old West'-themed wine bar specializes in barbecue and big reds and also pours rare whiskey and beer. Housed in a historic brick building from the mid-1800s, this is a rustic, all-American experience: raw-edge wooden tables, black leather stools and giant slabs of meat. The beer-can chicken sees a whole bird famously and photogenically served atop a can of beer. Bounty Hunter could feel kitschy, but the brisket

Cadet

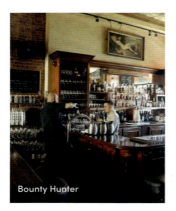
Bounty Hunter

is excellent and thanks to its three-decade-strong retail shop, which gets some of the highest allocations of the most sought-after Napa Valley wines in the world, you can find rare and small-lot Cabernets that make sense of all the smoke and fat.

bountyhunterwinebar.com

Bar Lucia
610 First Street #19

Located in the Oxbow Public Market – an indoor, year-round market with a beautiful wrap-around patio that serves up views of the Napa River – Bar Lucia was founded by the owner of the beloved Kara's Cupcakes, which has a stand next door. The seriously thoughtful and delightful selection of wines is intended to pair with the fresh sandwiches, salads and housemade dips, making it an ideal lunch or brunch spot. Hence, the wines, too, are fresh and lively – mostly by small producers in Napa Valley and Sonoma, with plenty of bubbles and rosé. There is also a selection of Instagram-friendly fresh fruit Frosés and Spritzes, but don't let that frighten you: it's just another a great reason to visit The Oxbow – a place where you are likely to overhear winemakers discussing barrel regimens and brix levels.

barlucia.com

Wine Bar at Copia
CIA at Copia (The Culinary Institute of America at Copia), 500 First Street

The expansive Copia educational centre, just across the river from downtown (by the Oxbow Market), was originally built by the Mondavis in 2001 and houses two theatres, a demonstration culinary kitchen, multiple classrooms and a full-service restaurant. It was mostly vacant for a number of years before the Culinary Institute of America (CIA) purchased the building and adjacent culinary garden in 2015. Now the vibrant set-up includes a state-of-the-art wine tasting bar where you can sample 24 wines from Napa Valley and beyond in 2-6 oz self-dispensed pours. It's most fun when explored as a group, so that you

ar Lucia

Where winemakers dine

We've been spending some time at **Bottega**. It's great for grilled polpo (octopus), shaved Brussels sprouts and fried calamari. The spaghetti alla Sophia Loren is always good. Meat, fish, anything goes. Ibérico pork is one of the specials, cooked sort-of-rare like a steak. And sometimes there's a special with truffles and pasta. Don't miss the tableside pasta, where they put some whiskey in a wheel of cheese and cook the pasta or spaghetti in it – that's gorgeous.

There's Italian wine, of course – Barolo – and a good list of Napa Cabs. Sometimes we have Champagne. There's all kinds of dessert – donuts with apple compote, tiramisu, cheese – and they have a great bar.

**Benoit Touquette,
Fait-Main Wines**

Self-dispensing pourers, Wine Bar at C...

can compare wines and then explore the museum, a home to rare specimens that showcase Napa Valley's expansive history as a winemaking region.

ciaatcopia.com/wine-bar

Carpe Diem
1001 2nd Street Suite #185

Strategically located on one of the most charming corners of a city that has many charming

Culinary Institute of America (CIA)

corners, Carpe Diem opened in 2010 and has attracted and maintained a loyal following thanks to its consistently good food and warm hospitality. The original brick building that houses this cosy wine bar and restaurant nearly collapsed in the 2014 earthquake that shook downtown; thankfully, it has been restored and continues to thrive. Boasting a full cocktail list and a Mediterranean-inspired dinner menu, the bar is a cheerful place for a casual evening, while the white tablecloth dining room makes for a romantic dinner destination. The wine list isn't super-extensive but it's user-friendly and fairly priced. Expect local favourites and familiar international selections, from Champagne and Sancerre to Langhe Nebbiolo.

carpediemnapavalley.com

The terrace, Carpe Diem

Downtown Napa tasting rooms

A peculiarly Californian concept, winery tasting rooms have blossomed in downtown Napa. Within a few blocks of this vibrant town an hour north of the Golden Gate Bridge, you can explore a dozen wineries in cool, relaxed spaces.

Gamling & McDuck

Unlike in most European wine regions, where one would visit the winery itself to get a flavour of the wine firsthand, in California tasting rooms serve as a way to experience not just the wine but also the brand when an on-site visit is out of the question. Many small producers work out of co-op or 'custom crush' facilities, which either don't have the resources to welcome guests or simply don't allow it (with a different permit required in the USA to pour wine, which can be costly). Some of these estates are in remote locations, too – and it's also worth noting that many wineries are, well, just not that sexy. A well-designed downtown space makes for a better and more convenient showcase.

'Tasting rooms serve as a way to experience not just the wine but also the brand when an on-site visit is out of the question'

Big wine brands like Mondavi and Buena Vista have made an urban home for themselves here, but you'll also find wines made with unusual grape varieties in more remote places, where tasting experiences would be logistically prohibitive.

Gone are the days of natural wine vs classic wine: now, carbonic Gamay and sparkling Counoise are served effortlessly alongside bold Howell Mountain Cabernet. One winemaker started adding organic oranges to her Chardonnay on a whim and now serves a Blood Orange Spritz on draught alongside her Burgundian varietal wines. Tasting rooms represent not just the super-wealthy and big wine brands, but small family- and minority-owned businesses that have been hustling to make the wine and life of their dreams in Napa Valley; many are there pouring for guests in person. Some tasting rooms encourage customers to bring their kids, their dogs, even their own vinyl records. Whimsical names, creative branding, wines of all colours and price points... these bricks-and-mortar spaces feel warm and personal, and when the winemaker is doing the pouring, the experience is even better.

Where winemakers dine

My current go-to spot in the valley is **Charlie's** in St Helena. Chef Elliot Bell and his team have created a convivial space with innovative takes on familiar dishes and an emphasis on local sourcing. You are almost guaranteed to spot a winemaker or three eating at the bar on any given night. Their cocktail programme is on-point and the wine list is just the right mix of local and international to find a pairing for every palate. My ideal evening begins with the shrimp cocktail and a Martini, graduates to the buttermilk fried chicken paired with a glass of Schramsberg blanc de blancs and ends with the campfire pie – the chef's take on the Cindy Pawlcyn classic with marshmallows and chocolate. If s'mores aren't for you, and if they're in season, be sure to order the blueberries and cream, with Howell Mountain berries grown by Matteo Abreu.

Jessica Koga, Schramsberg Vineyards

The River Club Napa
101 S. Coombs St. Unit 8

Located in a warehouse space that was originally a tannery and most recently, a brewery, The River Club Napa's industrial setting is made doubly charming by its location overlooking the Napa River. High-ceilinged and filled with light, the cheery space is pet- and kid-friendly. The by-appointment-only tasting room is shared by two young family-owned wine brands: Paper Planes and Belong Wine Co. A word of warning though: you won't find a single Cabernet Sauvignon on offer. Belong Wine Co. focuses on high-elevation, esoteric reds crafted from the likes of Mourvèdre and Cinsault and made with a 'light touch', while the main focus of Paper Planes is Pinot Noir from nearby Sonoma County, served as a refreshing rosé, a sparkling 'Pet Nat' and a still red.

exploretock.com/riverclubnapa

The River Club

Robert Mondavi Arch & Tower

Robert Mondavi Arch & Tower
930 3rd St.

Mondavi has found a more-than-suitable (albeit temporary) home for its robust hospitality offerings while the iconic up-valley winery undergoes a lengthy renovation. Tastings at the near-10,000 sq ft (930m^2) Borreo building – built in 1877, with stones quarried from nearby Soda Canyon – range from an introductory flight of the Mondavi range to an immersive (and pricey) flight of Cabernet Sauvignon from the legendary To Kalon vineyard, including rare wines from Schrader and Double Diamond. This beautiful building, in the centre of downtown on the Napa River, is a wonderful place in which to experience these important and legendary wines.

robertmondaviwinery.com/pages/arch-and-tower

Gamling & McDuck
1420 2nd St.

Founder and Winemaker Adam McClary focuses on Cabernet Franc and Chenin Blanc, the great red and white of the Loire Valley, made from incredible terroirs. It's no surprise that the wines are serious, given that McClary has worked for Napa legends like Mayacamas, Bond and Harlan, but the comic book-like labels, designed by McClary, remind imbibers not to take the wine itself too seriously – as does the Renaissance meets punk-inspired tasting

Gamling & McDuck

room décor, a space that was also designed by McClary and where you will likely find him behind the bar. Best of all, an introductory tasting of three wines is complimentary (but please, buy a bottle).

gamlingandmcduck.com

Brown Estate
1005 Coombs Street

The Brown family purchased, rehabilitated and planted grapes in the eastern hills of Napa in 1980 and launched their first estate wine, a Zinfandel for which the family is still most famous, in 1996. Since then, the three siblings and proprietors have expanded their vineyard sourcing, varieties and brands, founding The House of Brown, a brand focused on regenerative farming and inclusivity. This downtown tasting room followed shortly after, opening in 2017. Here, the focus is on the core Brown lineup, primarily single-vineyard Zinfandel, as well as wines driven by Cabernet Sauvignon and fruit from the family's original estate. Glasses can be paired with cheese and charcuterie.

brownestate.com

The Wine Thief
708 First Street

This 'tasting collective' founded in 2015 offers flights of wine at the bar every day for walk-ins or during guided tastings by appointment. Featuring 'underground labels', the list being poured here is an eclectic mix of garagistes and established

Brown Estate

The Wine Thief

vignerons. Discover everything from Buoncristiani, made by three brothers who grew up tending their neighbour's vines and making wine with their father in the family garage, to Correlation, a second label for Vineyard 7&8 from Martha McClellan, who made wine at Harlan and Merryvale and is further exploring the terroir of Spring Mountain. Be sure to ask about the allocated wines of Purlieu and Le Pich – a personal project of the famous French consultant Julien Fayard.

twtnapa.com

Benevolent Neglect
1417 Second Street

Visitors of Benevolent Neglect are encouraged to BYOV ('bring your own vinyl') to share during tastings, so the loungey, retro vibe shouldn't come as a surprise. It's also unsurprising, given the name, that Benevolent Neglect specializes in minimal-intervention winemaking. The offering is varied – ranging from single-vineyard Cabernet to Vermentino to sparkling rosé. 'Drink it & Like it' instructs the fluorescent script above the bar. And while you're up, can you flip the record?

bnwines.com

Chateau Buena Vista
1142 First Street

How did a historic Sonoma winery known for rustic red field blends come to have a tasting room featuring Champagne and caviar in downtown Napa? It's all thanks to the famously charming and charismatic Burgundian wine mogul Jean-Charles Boisset, who purchased and restored Buena Vista winery in 2011. While the original winery is still a must-visit for history buffs (and possibly, too, for ghost

Where winemakers dine

The **Charter Oak** was created by Christopher Kostow, a mad genius and one of the youngest Michelin three-star chefs ever. The food here is simple and well made, with many ingredients coming from the farm located less than a mile from the restaurant.

Bouchon is a classic French Bistro dropped in the middle of Napa Valley. Owned by culinary celebrity Thomas Keller, he brings his mastery of French cuisine to a classic bistro environment.

Ray Ray's Tacos is the place to go for tacos reimagined by Culinary Institute of America graduate Rachel 'Ray Ray' Williams. Ray Ray worked at the Restaurant at Meadowood before finding her true calling in her love for traditional Texas street tacos. This restaurant in downtown St Helena is open for breakfast, lunch and dinner.

Aaron Pott, Pott Wine

hunters), outside of Sonoma, this art deco-style tasting room in the heart of downtown caters to the bon vivant with sparkling wine and caviar, Cabernet and bonbons.

buenavistawinery.com
chateau-buena-vista-napa

No Love Lost Wine Co.
960 Clinton Street

Founded in 2019 by Jay Nunez, a California-born first-generation Cuban American and former musician, 'Napa's premier all-natural winery' serves classic grape varieties like Cabernet, Merlot and Zinfandel from hailed terroirs in Rutherford and Howell Mountain alongside (without conflict or irony, and for a modest tasting fee) a chillable red featuring Counoise and a skin-fermented Picpoul. A lot of things are polarising in the world right now, but not the wines at No Love Lost. And thank goodness for that.

nolovelost.wine

Vin en Noir
1001 Caymus Street

Founded by television celebrity chef and restaurant owner Leilani Baugh, who is known for her signature 'Casian' cuisine (a fusion of Creole and Asian flavours and an homage to her grandmothers), Vin en Noir is committed to pouring wines

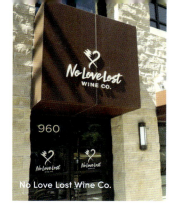

No Love Lost Wine Co.

exclusively from minority- and woman-owned wineries. The wines are as diverse and distinctive as those behind their creation, with at least 20 drops on offer at a time, many of which are small production and poured exclusively here. Everything is offered either by the glass or in customized flights, so there is plenty to explore. This energetic and welcoming space also hosts special weekend brunches and a 'sip and paint' class at its large communal table.

vinennoir.com

Mommenpop/Poe Wines
920 Franklin Street

If you're suffering from Cabernet palate fatigue (and that's OK – they are called 'Big Napa Reds' for a reason), Mommenpop is exactly what you need. Founder Samantha Sheehan (below) – who was already well known for both the quality of her Burgundy-inspired wine label, Poe, and for her spirit of collaboration and open-mindedness in the Napa Valley community – 'discovered' Mommenpop when she threw some just-picked Seville oranges into a small vat of freshly harvested Chardonnay. Try it for yourself in a light, bright tasting room where Mommenpop aperitifs are pouring, as well as Poe's limited production still and sparkling wines made from Chardonnay, Pinot Noir and Pinot Meunier (from the oldest PM vines in California).

mommenpop.com/pages/tasting-room

Vin en Noir

Mommenpop creator Samantha Sheehan

Glossary

Acidity The fresh, tart, often citrus-flavoured character of a wine, sensed along the sides of the tongue. Good acidity can signify ageing potential

Alluvial fan Triangle-shaped deposit of gravel, sand and silty sediment on the side of a hill or canyon (see Benchland)

AVA American Viticultural Area – the rough equivalent of a European appellation

Barrel A wooden container for storing and ageing wine, made of wooden staves bound in iron hoops; usually oak; in the standard size of 225 litres it is called a barrique in much of Europe

Benchland Fertile sloping soil deposits composed of run-off from mountain streams, usually alluvial fans. Famous benchland in Napa Valley is in the foothills of the Mayacamas range running through St Helena, Oakville, Rutherford and Yountville

Brix Brix (commonly used in the USA), Baumé (most of Europe) and Oechsle (Austria and Germany) are measurements of sugar and therefore potential alcohol in the wine. Napa Valley Cabernet is typically harvested at 23-25 Brix (12.8 degrees Baumé) which will give 13.6% alcohol by volume (ABV)

Cave A cellar, in Napa Valley often dug into the side of a hill

Clone A cutting or bud taken from a vine; a second plant genetically identical to the first. Many Napa Valley vineyards were (in a story since become myth) started with so-called 'suitcase clones' – budwood taken from European vines and smuggled back home

Crush The crushing of the grapes after picking; by extension, the harvest season

Cult wines 1990s term, now fallen into disuse, to describe the 'first growths' of Napa Valley – Harlan, Bryant Family, Colgin, Screaming Eagle and other small-batch, ultra-expensive wines

Diurnal shift The difference between day- and night-time temperatures. In July in Napa Valley this can be from 30°C to 10°C,

the cool nights vital for retaining acidity

Enologist (US), oenologist (Eur) A winemaker specializing in the scientific process of the creation of wine

Field blend A mix of grape varieties from one vineyard, vinified together. Common in 19th century Europe to ensure a crop if some varieties failed. Some old Napa Valley and more Sonoma vineyards are field blends

Filtration Passing wine through a mesh to remove particles that cause cloudiness; stabilizes the wine but also makes it less interesting in the opinion of some people

Fining Removing particles and impurities by adding a fining agent such as egg white, which binds with the particles and allows them to be removed by settling or filtration

Fumé Blanc Term was coined by Robert Mondavi in the late 1960s for barrel-aged Sauvignon Blanc; deliberately not trademarked to allow its use by all

Glass Fire The September 2020 wildfire that devastated Napa Valley and Sonoma (see Tubbs Fire)

Hang time Leaving grapes on the vine to accumulate sugars; uncommon now but popular in the late 1990s and early 2000s when big, ripe wines were in style

Indigenous yeast, wild yeast, native yeast Yeast that occurs naturally on grape skins, in the air of the vineyard and in the winery. Natural, wild or spontaneous yeast ferments are less predictable than 'cultured' yeast ferments and can result in wines of more complexity and flavour

Judgement of Paris, Paris Tasting Steven Spurrier's 1976 blind tasting of fine Bordeaux and Burgundy against California in which the latter came out top, a result that reverberates today

Mayacamas Mountains Part of the California Coastal Range, forming the border between Napa Valley and Sonoma Valley AVAs. Diamond Mountain and Mount Veeder are the northern and southern ends of the range in Napa Valley

Mediterranean climate Characterized

by long growing seasons with moderate to warm temperatures, damp winters and dry spring and summer seasons. Associated with areas around the Mediterranean basin; ideal for wine but with the (increasing) hazards of drought and wildfire

Microclimate A small area (anything from a single plot to a few hectares) with climatic differences distinct from the immediate surrounds

Mission vines The first vines introduced by Catholic missionaries to Mexico in the 1400s and later to California. Later identified as the red Listán Prieto from Castilla-La Mancha in Spain

Nested AVA An AVA that is part of another AVA; there are 17 nested AVAs within the Napa Valley AVA

Oak Used for barrels throughout the winemaking world; there are subtle differences between American and French oak, namely in the width of the grain and its subsequent effect on the wine

Onasatis Native Americans believed to have settled in Napa around 2000BCE; called Wappo (derived from 'guapo' meaning 'handsome' or 'brave') by Spanish settlers

Organic A wine made from organically grown grapes without added sulphites (USA); definition varies between countries

Parcel Selection, *Selection Parcellaire* Wine made with grapes from a particular plot within a vineyard

Phylloxera Sap-sucking aphid native to North America which lives on vine roots and leaves; introduced to Europe in the mid-c19th and destroyed almost all European vineyards. Still prevalent but controlled

Prohibition The Volstead Act prohibiting the manufacture and sale of alcoholic beverages took effect in the USA in 1920 and was repealed in 1933

Reserve Denotes an aged or special cuvée but (unlike in most of Europe) the term has no legal definition or meaning

Parkerization Term now hardly used to denote the prevalence of the kind of wine that Robert Parker was supposed to favour: rich, forward-fruited and high in alcohol

Rutherford Dust Term coined by André Tchelistcheff to describe the unique tannic characteristic of Rutherford wines: a combination of minerality, fine-dusted cocoa powder and silky palate

Smoke taint Only partially understood effect of wildfire smoke on grapes. Depending on ripeness, and length of exposure, can give wine the smell and taste of damp ashtrays

Stagecoach Vineyard One of the world's great vineyards, over 1,300 acres (500ha) of rocky, volcanic terroir from Pritchard Hill to Atlas Peak. Now owned by Gallo and used by hundreds of wineries, 25 of which make a vineyard-designate wine

Tannin Compounds found in grape skins, seeds and stems (and in oak), contributing to the structure, texture, and ageing potential of wine, especially red wine

Terroir The magical combination of soil, aspect, climate and winemaker which goes to make a wine. Warren Winiarski, founder of Stag's Leap Wine Cellars, called it 'The three G's – ground, grape and guy (or gal)'

To Kalon Napa Valley's legendary (and much fought-over) vineyard, first planted by HW Crabb in 1868. The name means 'highest beauty'; its grapes have gone into a roll-call of Napa Valley's most exalted wines

Tchelistcheff, André Russian emigré hired by Georges de Latour in 1938 to run Beaulieu Vineyard; the chain-smoking 'maestro', regarded as the most influential winemaker ever to work in Napa Valley, introduced methods such as small-lot vinification that are still in use today

Tubbs Fire One of the most destructive wildfires in California history, the October 2017 blaze started in Calistoga and devastated the city of Santa Rosa

UC Davis Important winemaking course at University of California, Davis – the equal of the universities of Bordeaux, Adelaide, Geisenheim and Stellenbosch

Vaca Mountains Part of the California Coastal Range, running along the eastern edge of Napa County and the Napa Valley AVA, with Howell Mountain to the north and Atlas Peak to the south

Further reading

Wine

The Winemaker's Dance: Exploring Terroir in the Napa Valley, Jonathan Swinchatt and David G. Howell, University of California Press 2004
A must for anyone looking for a deeper understanding of the natural conditions that make Napa Valley a world-class wine region.

The Wines of California, Elaine Chukan Brown, Academie du Vin Library 2025
A journey through California by one of the foremost experts on the region, with major sections on Napa Valley as well as introducing readers to exciting lesser-known regions.

Napa Valley Then and Now, Kelli A White, Rudd Press 2015
Kelli White is one of Napa's most accomplished sommeliers and writers. Over 200 wineries exhaustively profiled and thousands of wines tasted. 1,200 pages and over $200 for used copies. A must for any Napa Valley completist.

Biography

Harvests of Joy: How the Good Life Became a Great Business, Robert Mondavi, Harcourt Brace 1999
The architect of modern Napa Valley tells his story from childhood to Napa Valley titan, warts and all.

Reflections of a Vintner: Stories and Seasonal Wisdom from a Lifetime in Napa Valley, Tor Kenward, Cameron Books 2022
The epicurean life of a Napa Valley veteran, 27 years at Beringer and now proprietor of the boutique Tor winery.

The House of Mondavi: The Rise and Fall of an American Wine Dynasty, Julia Flynn Siler, Gotham Books 2008
Meticulously researched book by a Wall Street Journal reporter delves into the Mondavis' complex family relationships and dynamics.

History

Judgment of Paris, California vs France and the historic 1976 Paris Tasting that revolutionized wine, George M Taber, Scribner 2005
The subtitle says it all: the official version from the only journalist in the room.

Napa: The Far Side of Eden, New Money, Old Land, and the Battle for Napa Valley James Conaway, Clarion 2003
In the follow-up to 1992's T*he Story of an American Eden*, Conaway claims the idyll has soured and corporate and vanity winemaking is wrecking Napa Valley's environment. The book got him banned from many wineries and institutions. The third in the trilogy is *Napa at Last Light: America's Eden in an Age of Calamity.*

The Silverado Squatters, Robert Louis Stevenson, Aegypan 2005 (first published 1884)
Napa Valley's most famous adopted son on his Napa Valley honeymoon adventures. Stevenson wrote part of the book at what is now Schramsberg; some of his notes provided the descriptive detail for the scenery in *Treasure Island.*

We are the Land: A History of Native California, Damon B Akins and William J Bauer, University of California Press 2021
An exploration of the indigenous peoples who stewarded and shaped California,

and how Western exploration and the Gold Rush changed their lives.

Hidden History of Napa Valley, Alexandria Brown, History Press 2019
Little-known stories about the Chinese community that once thrived in Napa Valley.

Culinary

A New Napa Cuisine, Christopher Kostow, Ten Speed Press 2014
The Michelin-starred chef of Meadowood, Charter Oak and Loveski deli on his
journey from San Diego to St Helena, and the recipes he created along the way.

Mustard's Grill Napa Valley Cookbook, Cindy Pawlcyn, Ten Speed Press 2001
Recipes from a Napa Valley institution. For more than 30 years Cindy Pawlcyn has
been catering to locals at the eatery they call 'the fancy rib joint with way too
many wines'.

The French Laundry Cookbook, Thomas Keller, Artisan 1999
You'll probably never cook a recipe but you'll love the gorgeous food and behind-
the-scenes shots at one of the world's most famous restaurants.

The Vineyard Kitchen: Menus Inspired by the Seasons, Maria Helm Sinskey,
William Morrow & Co 2003
Chef and vintner Maria Helm Sinskey shares tips and recipes for cooking with
California's bounty season by season.

**The Model Bakery Cookbook: 75 Favorite Recipes from the Beloved Napa Valley
Bakery**, Karen Mitchell and Sarah Mitchell Hansen, Chronicle 2013
Another Napa Valley institution, the Model Bakery has been in the same location
in St Helena for nearly a century; Karen Mitchell has owned it for three decades.

The Essential Napa Valley Cookbook, Jess Lander, Pediment Publishing 2024
Iconic recipes from top restaurants and chefs: Gott's Ahi Burger, Bounty Hunter's
Beer Can Chicken, Mustards' Mighty Meatloaf, Charlie Palmer Steak's Lobster
Corn Dogs, and Model Bakery's Chocolate Rads Cookies.

Fiction

Drunk on Love, Jasmine Guillory, Headline Eternal 2022
A Black woman inherits a Napa winery and finds love. 'The spicy scenes were
definitely hot enough for my taste, although I didn't get quite enough swoon.' –
The Feminist Book Club.

A Walk in the Clouds, Deborah Chiel, Penguin 1995
A soldier, deserted by his wife, dreads going back home after World War II. But his
life changes instantly when he meets a woman crying by the side of the road.

Vintage, Anita Clay Kornfeld, iUniverse 2007
Adventures and family drama unfolds after an Italian immigrant comes to the Napa
Valley in 1894 with his wife and several sons.

Trial by Fire, Danielle Steel, Macmillan 2024
On a visit to Napa Valley a Frenchwoman finds herself struggling to escape the
wildfires. Topical, from one the the world's bestselling writers.

Gatsby's Vineyard, AE Maxwell, HarperCollins 1993
'Napa Valley, where wine and blood ripened in the sunshine...' Dark goings-on
investigated by a husband and ex-wife duo.

Index

Accendo Cellars 114
accommodations 13, 97, 101, 104, 136–47
acidity 9, 13
Adamvs 127
air travel 86
Albariño 29
alluvial fans 35
alluvial soil 9, 34
American Canyon 70
American rootstock 18
American Viticultural Areas see AVAs
Angèle Restaurant & Bar (Napa) 156, 160
Araujo 26
Araujo, Bart and Daphne 114
Arkenstone 93
art galleries 13, 108–9
Atlas Peak 45–6
AVA system 9, 37–8
AVAs 36–53

B Cellars 177
Bale Grist Mill State Historic Park 106
Barrett, Bo 64–5
Barrett, Heidi 26, 66, 67, 150
Barrett, Jim 64
Beaulieu Vineyard 18, 19, 20, 23, 37
Becker, Scott 113
Bella Oaks 96
Bella Union 95
benchland 9, 43, 44
Benevolent Neglect (Napa) 197
Beringers 19, 20
Biagi, Tony 98
bike tours 87
Bond 99
boom years 16–18
Booth, Suzanne Deal 95, 96

Bothe-Napa Valley State Park 104, 106
Brion 118
Brounstein, Al and Adele 22
Brown Estate (Napa) 196
Bunny Foo-Foo 106–7
Burgess Cellars 92
bus travel 87
BV 13

Cabernet Franc 29, 55, 58–9
Cabernet Sauvignon 17, 26, 37, 54, 55, 58
CADE Estate 91
Cain Vineyard 28
Cakebread Cellars 174–5
Calistoga 73–4
    accommodations 97, 101, 137–8
    elite wineries 113–14
    restaurants 93, 100–1, 150–1
    things to do 105–6
    tours and tastings 126–7
    wine bars 184–5
    winery restaurants 172–3
Calistoga AVA 38–9
Calistoga Depot 106
Calistoga Inn 150
car rental 86
Cardinale 99
Carneros see Los Carneros
Castello di Amorosa 74, 105
Cathiard Vineyard 130
Caymus 15, 17
    Cabernet Sauvignon 1978 66
Chappellet, Donn and Molly 22, 63
Chappellet Winery 91,

131–2
Cabernet Sauvignon 1969 63
Chardonnay 13, 26, 37, 54, 55–6
Charles Krug Winery 21, 22, 55
Charlie's (St Helena) 72, 194
Charter Oak (St Helena) 72, 93, 134, 152
Chateau Buena Vista (Napa) 197–8
Chateau Montelena 25, 97
    Chardonnay 1973 24, 64–5
Chenin Blanc 29
Chiles Valley District 40–1
climate 9, 13, 31
    changing 31
    when to visit 79–80
Clos du Bal 100
Cole's Chop House (Napa) 154–5, 174
Colgin Cellars 26, 91
communion wine 19
Continuum Estate 91
Cook (St Helena) 72, 154
Coombs, Nathan 16
Coombsville 13, 16, 51–2, 120–1
Copia 13, 108, 188
Coppola, Francis Ford 17, 95, 131
Corison, Cathy 28, 98, 128
Corison Winery 28, 98, 128–9
Counoise 29
Covert Estate 120–1
Crabb, Henry Walker 17–18
Crystal Springs 38, 43, 92
Culinary Institute of

America at Copia 108, 188
Culinary Institute of America at Greystone 107
cult wineries 9
cycling 87

Dalla Valle, Naoko and Gustav 66
Dalla Valle Vineyards 9, 99
Maya Proprietary Red Blend 1992 26, 66
Daniel, John Jr 20
Darioush 13, 135, 177–8
Davies, Jack and Jamie 22
Davis Estates 172
de Latour, Georges 20
DePuy, Joanne 24
Detert Family Vineyards 117
di Rosa Center for Contemporary Art 13, 109
Diamond Creek 22, 92
Diamond Mountain District 16, 22, 39, 92–3
diurnal shift 9, 13, 34
Domaine Carneros 178–81
Domaine Chandon 132, 149
Donum Estate 109, 181
Dunn Vineyards 92

elevation 13
elite wineries, visiting 13, 112–21
Erickson, Andy 13, 121
Exposto, Jason 116

Far Niente 95
Favia, Annie 13, 121, 144
Favia Estate 13, 121
festivals 80–5
fluvial soil 34
food 13

see also festivals; restaurants
Frank Family Vineyards 96
Frank, Rich and Leslie 96
Freemark Abbey 19
French Laundry (Yountville) 71, 126, 149, 152–3
Futo Estate 99, 116

Gallagher, Patricia 23, 24
Gamling & McDuck (Napa) 195–6
Garnett, Tom 117
Gentleman Farmer (Napa) 178
geography 30–5
geology 34–5
Gold Rush 16
Goose & Gander (St Helena) 72, 144
Grace Family Vineyards 66
Graham, Spencer 64
grape varieties 29, 54–61
Grgich, Mike 22, 25
Groth Reserve Cabernet Sauvignon 1985 26

Hall Wines 106–7
hang time 27
Harlan, Bill 115
Harlan Estate 9, 26, 91, 99
Heintz, Charles 18
Heitz Cellar 22, 28, 37
Martha's Vineyard Cabernet Sauvignon 1974 65
Heitz, Joe and Alice 21–2, 55
Hermosa 17
Herrera, Rolando 174
Hess Persson Estates Winery and Art Museum 108–9
historic wines 62–7

history 9, 14–29
home winemaking 19
hot air balloons 102
hotels 13, 97, 101, 104, 136–47
Hourglass 98
Howell Mountain 40, 91–2, 127
Hudson Ranch & Vineyards 135
Hundred Acre 27
Hyde de Villaine (HdV) 94

immigrants, European 14, 16, 19
indigenous peoples 14
Inglenook 17, 18, 37, 95, 130–1
Cabernet Sauvignon 1941 63
itineraries 90–109
Downtown Napa on foot 102–4
Icons and legends 97–101
Mountain wineries 91–3
Valley floor 94–7

Jesuits 15
Johnson, Artie 160
Joseph Phelps Vineyards 98, 173–4
Judgement of Paris 9, 23–5, 37, 64, 97

Keller, Thomas 71, 149, 152, 168, 198
Kenzo Restaurant (Napa City) 126, 157
Kinsman, Nigel 95, 114, 184
Koga, Jessica 194
Krug, Charles 16, 19, 47, 125

La Cave de la Madeleine (Paris) 23

La Sirena Winery 127–8
LOLA 126
Long, Zelma 23
Los Carneros
  accommodations
  146–7
  AVA 53
  things to do 109
  tours and tastings 135
  winery restaurants
  178–81
Louis M. Martini Winery
  96
  Private Reserve
  California Mountain
  Barbera 1970 64

McCoy, Carlton 13
McCrea, Fred 9, 20
McDonald Vineyards 115
Malbec 61
Martini, Louis 19, 20
Martini, Mike 64
Matthiasson, Steve and
  Jill 27–8, 134
Matthiasson Winery
  134–5
May, Cliff 22
Mayacamas Mountains
  35, 91
Mayacamas Vineyards 93
medicinal wine 19
Melka Estates 114–15
Melka, Philippe and
  Cherie 114, 134
Merlot 60–1
méthode champenoise 22
Mexico 15
Mission vines 15, 18
missionaries 15
mom-and-pop farms 9
Mommenpop/Poe Wines
  (Napa) 199
Mondavi family 19,
  21, 22
Mondavi, Peter 21, 22
Mondavi, Robert 21,
  22–3, 37, 116
Mondavi, Robert Jr 126

Mondeuse 17
Mount Veeder 48–9,
  108–9, 118–19, 133
Mt Brave 133
museums 71, 108–9, 162

Napa City 16, 69–70
  accommodations 104,
  144–6
  restaurants 104, 154–7
  tasting rooms 192–9
  things to do 108
  walking itinerary
  102–4
  wine bars 186–91
  wine shops 164–8
  winery restaurants 178
Napa River 34, 69
Napa Valley
  geography 30–5
  history 9, 14–29
  itineraries 90–109
  map 10–11
Napa Valley Museum
  (Yountville) 71, 108
Nickel & Nickel 95
Niebaum, Gustave 17, 20
No Love Lost Wine Co.
  (Napa) 198

Oak Knoll District 49,
  133–5, 177–8
Oakville 95
  AVA 44–5, 99
  elite wineries 115–17
  things to do 107
  tours and tastings 131
  wine shops 161–2
  winery restaurants 177
Oakville Grocery 107,
  161–2
Old Faithful Geyser of
  California 74, 75, 106
Onasatis 15
Opus One 13, 99, 116–17
OVID 119–20
Oxbow Public Market
  (Napa) 102, 108

Pahlmeyer 26
Paris Exposition (1889) 18
Parker, Robert M. Jr 9,
  25–6, 27, 66, 67
Peschon, Françoise 114
Peterson, Austin 119
Petite Sirah 61
Phelps, Chris 154
Phillips, Jean 67
phylloxera 9, 18
Pine Ridge Vineyards
  100
Pinot Gris 57
Pinot Noir 58
PlumpJack Estate
  Winery 99
Pott, Aaron 118, 198
Pott Wine 118–19
prehistory 15
Pressler, Elizabeth 64
Pride Mountain
  Vineyards 92
Pritchard Hill 22, 38,
  49–51, 91
  elite wineries 119–20
  tours and tastings
  131–2
Prohibition 9, 18–19,
  20, 37
Promontory 99, 115

Quintessa 99
Quixote Winery 132

Raymond, Roy 20
Raymond Vineyards 20
Realm Cellars 113
red grapes 58–61
restaurants 93, 96–7,
  100–1, 104, 148–57
  winery 170–81
Riesling 17, 29, 55
River Club Napa 194
Robert Biale Vineyards
  133–4
Robert Mondavi Arch &
  Tower (Napa) 82, 195
Robert Mondavi Winery
  22, 37

Cabernet Sauvignon 1974 65–6
Rothschild, Baron Philippe de 116
Round Pond Estate 175
Rudd Estate 99, 131
Rutherford 20, 43–4, 94–5
  accommodations 101, 140–3
  tours and tastings 130–1
  winery restaurants 174–7
Rutherford Grill 150

St. Helena 13, 72–3
  accommodations 139–40
  AVA 42–3
  elite wineries 114–15
  restaurants 93, 101, 151–2
  things to do 106–7
  tours and tastings 127–30
  wine bars 185–6
  wine shops 160–1
  winery restaurants 173–4
San Andreas fault 35
San Francisco Earthquake 18
Sauvignon Blanc 56
Scarecrow 27
Schrader 26
Schram, Jacob 16, 22
Schramsberg Vineyards 22, 97, 126–7
Screaming Eagle 9, 26, 99
  Cabernet Sauvignon 1992 67
Semillon 57
Sequoia Grove 175–7
settlers 15
Shafer Vineyards 100, 133
shopping 158–69
Silverado Trail 100

smallpox 15
Smith, Jeff 98
Snowden Vineyards 28
soil 9, 13, 31, 34, 35
Sorenson Vineyard 92
Souverain 9, 21, 23
Spanish invaders 15
Spottswoode Winery 129
Spring Mountain District 41–2, 92–3
Spurrier, Steven 23, 24
Stags Leap District
  accommodations 101
  AVA 46–7
  tours and tastings 132–3
Stag's Leap Wine Cellars 25, 100
  SLV Cabernet Sauvignon 1973 24, 100
Starr, Pam 180
Steffens, Wesley 92
Sterling Vineyards 105
Stewart, Lee 9, 21
Stony Hill Vineyard 9, 13, 20, 28, 128
Sullivan Rutherford Estate 95
sustainability 27

Taber, George M. 24
Tamber Bey 172–3
tastings 13, 125–35
  Downtown Napa 102–4, 125, 192–9
Tchelistcheff, André 20, 22
tectonic plates 35
temperature 31
  day/night 9, 13, 34
Tempranillo 29
Terraces, The 94
terroir 31
To Kalon 17–18, 22, 91, 117
Togni, Philip 63
topography 31
Touquette, Benoit 190

towns 68–74
train travel 86–7
transportation 86–7
Tres Sabores 129–30

Vaca Mountains 35, 91
Vallejo, Mariano Guadalupe 15
Vin en Noir (Napa) 198–9
Vine Hill Ranch 91
Vineyard 7&8 92
Viognier 57
vitis vinifera 15, 18
volcanic activity 35
volcanic soil 9, 34
Volstead Act (1920) 18–19

walking trails 87
Wappo 15
Welcome to Napa Valley Sign 28–9, 107
Wheeler Farms 95, 173
white grapes 55–7
White Rock Vineyards 28
Wild Horse Valley 52
Wine Advocate, The 25
wine bars 182–91
wine shops 158–69
Wine Thief (Napa) 196–7
Wine Train 86–7
Winiarski, Warren 22–3, 25

Yount, George Calvert 15, 17, 47
Yountville 15, 71–2
  accommodations 97, 143–4
  AVA 47–8
  elite wineries 117–18
  restaurants 93, 96–7, 152–4
  things to do 108
  tours and tastings 132
  wine shops 162–4

Zinfandel 17, 59–60

Acknowledgements

The publishers have made every effort to trace the copyright holders of the text and images reproduced in this book. If, however, you believe that any work has been incorrectly credited or used without permission, please contact us immediately and we will endeavour to rectify the situation. Images of businesses are copyright of those businesses.

Cover, 3 Shutterstock/Jilko, 1 Napa Valley Vintners, 6-7 Quixote Winery, 8 Visit Napa Valley, 12-13 Napa Valley Vintners, 14-16 Napa County Historical Society, 17 historyofto-kalon.com, 19 US Library of Congress, 20-21 Napa County Historical Society, 21 Heitz Cellar, 22-23 Napa County Historical Society, 24 estate of Steven Spurrier, 25 Susana Raab, 26 Club Oenologique, 27 Steve Matthiasson, 28-29 Bob McClenahan/Visit Napa Valley, 30 Visit Napa Valley, 31 Napa Valley Insider, 32-33 Adobe Stock, 34 Peter Michael Winery, 35 Visit Napa Valley, 36 Adobe Stock, 38 napavalley.com, 39-43 Napa Valley Vintners, 43 pressdemocrat.com, 44 Napa Valley Vintners, 44 napavalley.com, 45 atlaspeak.com, 46 Napa Valley Vintners, 47 Visit Napa Valley, 48, 49 Napa Valley Vintners, 54 Bob McClenahan/Visit Napa Valley, 56, 59 Adobe Stock, 60 Visit Napa Valley, 61 Adobe Stock, 62, 67 Napa Valley Vintners, 68, 69 Adobe Stock, 70 Visit Napa Valley, 71 Shutterstock, 72, Janette Maack/Visit Napa Valley, 73, 74 Max Whittaker/Visit Napa Valley, 75 Rennet Stowe/Wikipedia Commons, 78 Adobe Stock, 81 Visit Napa Valley, 82, 84 Michael Cuffe/Visit Napa Valley, 85 John Troxall (Elle King) Flying Pig Studio (Napaulée), 86-87 Visit Napa Valley, 90 Adobe Stock, 96, 97, 101, 105, 106, 107 Visit Napa Valley, 109, 112 Club Oenologique, 115 St Helena Historical Society, Fine + Rare, 116 Wikipedia Commons, 120-121 Club Oenologique, 121 Visit Napa Valley, 122-123 Cliff Lede Vineyards, 124 melanderarchitects.com, 127 Visit Napa Valley, 127 Club Oenologique, 128 napavalley.com, 130-132, 135 Visit Napa Valley, 138 napavalley.com, 139 sthelena.com, 140 festivalnapa.com, 144 Fine + Rare, 145, 148, 150-151, 153, 154-155, 161 Visit Napa Valley, 162 yountville.com, 165 Downtown Napa, 166 Napa Wine Project, 169 Tybay Yabut, 173, 175, 177 Visit Napa Valley, 179 Gentleman Farmer/Michael Cuffe, 182 thesaintnapavalley. com, 183, 184 Visit Napa Valley, 186 erosion.buzz, 186, 187 Visit Napa Valley, 188 Napa Wine Project, 190 Visit Napa Valley, 191 Downtown Napa, 192, 196 Visit Napa Valley, 196 Napa Wine Project, 197 Visit Napa Valley, 199 Napa Wine Project.